CLOSE CALL

by

Walter Kanitz

PaperJacks LTD.

Markham, Ontario, Canada

AN ORIGINAL CANADIAN

PaperJacks

One of a series of Canadian books
first published by PaperJacks Ltd.

CLOSE CALL

To Oskar
1899-1941

PaperJacks edition published April, 1979

This original PaperJacks edition is printed from brand-new plates
made from newly set, clear, easy-to-read type. No part of this
book may be reproduced or transmitted in any form or by any
means, electronic or mechanical, including photography, recording,
or any information storage or retrieval system, without permission
in writing from the publisher. PaperJacks editions are published
by PaperJacks Ltd., 330 Steelcase Road, Markham, Ontario
L3R 2M1.

CONTENTS

Prologue

The men stood lined up three rows deep. Two hundred of them. Some were old, a few still in their teens. Two heavy machine guns placed on the left and the right fringes of the market square made escape impossible.

The tall officer walked slowly down the first line of men scanning each face as he passed. Reaching the end he continued with the second line. When he reached me I looked into a pair of cold, pale blue eyes in a puffed-up, emotionless face, supported by a tunic collar much too tight for the fleshy neck. A bulge of fat squeezed from under the collar's rim, almost obscuring the silver double S of Hitler's Waffen SS.

I thought he hesitated for an instant as he faced me but it may have been my stoked-up imagination because he continued his inspection without hesitation and in silence.

Finished at last, he walked stiffly to the center of the square and bellowed a command to a younger officer, who immediately darted down the lines of men counting loudly from one to ten and yanking each tenth man from his row. At the end of the count some twenty men were standing in front of their former lines. Another sharp command and a bevy of steel-helmeted soldiers swept down on the selected men and marched them briskly from the square. The rest of us remained standing.

Time stood still. Five minutes may have passed, maybe fifty. The tension numbed all senses.

Then suddenly there was the staccato of a machine gun in the distance, followed by silence.

The tall officer counted off another twenty men to dig the graves.

The year was 1941. The locale: somewhere in occupied France.

1
Trouble

My brother was astride the chair, resting his elbows on its back in front of the small stage, watching two-dozen shapely legs move to the rhythm of a tinny piano. He was rehearsing a new review for the Simplicissimus, a small but popular cabaret in Vienna's inner core.

The room was dark except for the stage floodlights. Sitting at a table in the semidarkness I watched my brother's lean profile. He was eleven years older than I. We had never been as close as brothers are supposed to be but there was a bond of strong affection between us, although the difference in age always dominated our relationship. Compared to him I was still a boy in short pants interested mainly in soccer, while he had already slept with girls.

He sensed my presence and turned his head in my direction.

"Talk to you later," he shouted over the tinkle of the piano.

I was a frequent visitor to the cabaret and had watched many a rehearsal. Ordinarily I would have been pleasantly stimulated by the sexy legs and the girls' scantily covered breasts bobbing lively to the cadence of their dance steps, but this time the spectacle was lost on me. My mind wasn't in it. Too many disturbing things had happened earlier in the day.

It began with a short and laconic news bulletin over the radio in the morning announcing that Chancellor Schuschnigg, the head of the Austrian government, had just returned from a visit to Berchtesgaden, Hitler's mountain retreat, where he had conferred with the Fuehrer.

On the surface it seemed an innocuous event but in the context of the period there was a sinister tinge to it. No one had known of Schuschnigg's trip in the first place and the absence of any explanation for the chancellor's visit to Germany made the whole thing highly suspect. There had been too much secrecy.

The papers said the meeting between the two heads of state had been arranged "in the spirit of friendship and mutual understanding traditional in the relationship between Germany and Austria"—which was bloody nonsense. There hadn't been any such thing as understanding —let alone friendship—between the two countries ever since Hitler had come to power some five years before, in 1933. The border was virtually closed. German tourists who wanted to vacation in Austria had to pay a tax of one thousand marks. There was barbed wire along the border, and an army of renegade Nazis—the so-called Austrian Legion—held regular maneuvers on the other side ready to march into Austria at the drop of a hat. Hitler had made no secret of the fact that he considered Austria an integral part of his future empire. It was printed in black and white in his book *Mein Kampf*.

And now Austria's chancellor had been to Berchtesgaden. For what reason? Was this perhaps the beginning of the end for Austria? The thought was depressing. Who wanted to live under the Nazis?

On the other hand, could it be a bluff on Hitler's part? Blackmail, perhaps, for which he was so famous? It couldn't be anything else. I was sure he wouldn't risk a war with the Western Powers that had guaranteed Austria's independence. He was probably playing some sort of obscure diplomatic game for the purpose of blackmailing the West into making a few more political or economic concessions. He had done it before successfully. The more I thought of this possibility the more I was convinced it was the answer. This kind of intrigue had been going on for years. There was no danger. No cause for alarm. Nothing was going to change, I decided. Sitting there watching the rehearsal, I began to feel better.

While I was thinking I hadn't noticed Fritzi, who had slipped out of the darkness and was now sitting across the table from me. I discovered I wasn't alone when she opened her mouth to speak.

"What's the matter with you jerks today?" she asked. "You both act as if you were dead. You and that brother of yours."

I didn't explain. From past experience I knew it would be of no use. Fritzi, with the hourglass figure of a classical statue, was as dumb as she was beautiful. She wouldn't understand. She was my brother's latest acquisition and had already lasted an unprecedented six months as his mistress. She was his type. He loved glamour but hated brains in women. Brainy women meant trouble, he professed.

Although my depressed mood had evaporated, I was grateful to Fritzi for the diversion. It was amusing to listen to her. She began to explain that my brother was actually a dirty sonofabitch who exploited her without consideration for her needs. He had been rude, she said. Instead of buying her a lunch after she had been working like a horse rehearsing since early morning, he had given her some money and told her to buy a frankfurter or two for herself and to get off his back. That was no way to treat a woman who had sacrificed so much for him.

She didn't elaborate on the point of sacrifice but while she gesticulated to illustrate her complaint, her dressing gown popped open exposing a pair of breasts of rare beauty. I couldn't help looking. Full, round, with two oversized nipples which stood erect under her nervous agitation. Fritzi saw I was looking but did nothing to hide her breasts. She probably reasoned that I was her lover's brother and as such, a member of the family, so where was the problem?

The piano stopped. The dancers left the stage chattering. My brother came over to the table as Fritzi slowly covered up. It was obvious he was worried. It showed in his face and in the way he humped his shoulders.

"Anything new at your paper?" he asked.

He meant the evening paper for which I wrote a weekly column on youth, sports, and nightspots. I had been there earlier in the day and found the mood black. I heard the publisher had sent the office boy to have his passport renewed in a hurry and the publisher was a well-informed man. This could mean he was getting panicky. Maybe so, but I had already made up my mind by deciding there was no reason for concern. My brother's visible anxiety irritated me. I felt an urge to antagonize him. I wanted to prove to him he was wrong about Hitler. I wanted to be right.

"Not much," I said, "except everybody is shitting in his pants every time someone says 'Heil Hitler.' Much ado about nothing." It didn't bother me that my feelings hadn't been much different from his only a short time before, but he sensed there was something wrong with me and flared up.

"Stupid idiot!" he said. "You stupid little know-it-all. Always knowing everything better. Can't you talk like an intelligent human being just once?"

My bad mood came back as on cue.

"Christ," I said, "don't call me an idiot, because if I'm an idiot you're nothing but a scared old woman. Afraid of your own bloody shadow. You're as full of shit as everybody else!"

"Idiot," he repeated, "I don't know much about politics but you don't have to know much to see the whole thing stinks. Yes, it stinks. From A to Z. You understand? Am I getting through to you and your goddamned superiority? Or do you insist on being an idiot?"

"Shut up!" I said, getting up and grabbing my coat.

"Is that all you can say?" he asked. "Shut up? Is that the range of your intelligence? If so, I'm sorry for you.

10

And let me tell you something else: you can call me whatever you want, an old woman or full of shit or whatever, but mark my words: I give the whole thing thirty days. Thirty days—no more. In thirty days we will be a Nazi colony whether you bloody well like it or not!"

"You've flipped," I said. "Your perspective is gone. You're scared. Yes, scared and full of shit as you said yourself. Why don't you get all that crap out of your system? Jump in the hay with Fritzi. That'll do it!"

Fritzi liked the suggestion. It was written all over her face. I walked out.

Outside, there was a brisk breeze. The winter air cooled my face but I felt miserable again. I was sorry I had let myself be sucked into that childish scene and I knew I had lied to myself trying to fit the facts to my own wishful thinking. My artificial optimism was shrinking, and not just because of the fight with my brother. There had been something else earlier in the day which I had discounted as unimportant. Now I didn't think it was unimportant.

In midmorning, shortly after news of the chancellor's meeting had broken, I had gone to the office of the modest women's tabloid for which I wrote a children's page under the byline of Uncle Paul. It was amazing that the kids liked the stuff I wrote, and there was a small but regular paycheck which came in handy. It gave me a chance to work for my degree.

The editor sat behind his desk staring into space, a whole pile of unopened mail in front of him. He looked tired.

"Good morning," I said. "Anything wrong? You look sick."

He turned to look at me. He had once been one of the most distinguished newspapermen in Austria. An old man now, he had retired to the easier task of editing the small weekly in a chain of papers owned by the country's labor organizations.

"Yes," he said. "I am sick. Sick of Hitler."

"I saw the papers," I said, "and I heard the news. Is it that bad?"

He nodded.

The thought went through my mind that he was overly pessimistic. It's his age, I thought. He is an old man. Old people tend to overreact. He guessed my thoughts.

"You don't believe me," he said, "because you think I am an old man and scared. Yes, perhaps you are right. I am an old man and I am scared. I see a great deal of trouble. Perhaps I am wrong, but if I were you I would get out as quickly as I can. You can always come back if it turns out I was wrong."

"Aren't you exaggerating a little?" I said. "After all, the papers say it was harmless. Just a friendly exchange of ideas. Nothing to worry about."

He smiled sadly. "The papers," he said softly, "print only what they are being told to print—what the government wants them to print."

The room was silent. He stared straight out the window, deep in thought. "Yes," he said after a while, "if I were you I would be very careful. Very cautious. We are all on the Nazi blacklist. You know that."

"I know," I said. "But how about you? Why don't you go? With your political past you'll be one of the first they'll get."

He made a vague gesture with both hands.

"I am an old man. I have nothing to lose. Not much anyway. But you are young. I envy you. How old are you? Twenty? Twenty-two?"

"Twenty-four," I said, slightly annoyed. I had heard enough. "Here is my copy for next week." I threw the sheets on his desk.

Noticing my annoyance he gave me a look that indicated how hopeless it was to talk sense into a young moron.

I grinned.

"Cheer up," I said. "It isn't that bad. Hitler wouldn't dare." Strangely, I even believed it myself when I said it.

Out on the street the air smelled of snow. He is old, I thought. Old people are easily depressed. Much too prone to pessimism. No sense getting panicky over an exhibition of political shadow boxing which would be forgotten in another day or two. I was very sure of my assessment. Of course I couldn't know at the time that less than three months later the editor's wife would receive a parcel in the mail containing an urn wrapped in old newspapers. In the urn were his ashes. The parcel would come from one of the new concentration camps the Nazis had established in Austria. It was just as well I didn't know it at the time or it might have spoiled what was to become a pleasant evening.

I looked at my watch. Quarter to six. I could still catch Maria before she left the office where she worked. The advice I had given my brother before I stormed out of the cabaret would in all probability work as well for me as for him.

"Fuck them all," I thought, "Hitler, Schuschnigg, and my brother. To hell with them. I have to get it out of my system or I'll choke!"

I knew Maria would cooperate.

2

The Knock at Dawn

Nothing clears the cobwebs from a man's brain faster than a night with the woman he loves. Maria nuzzled the hair on my chest.

"You stink of sex and sin," she said, screwing up her nose into wrinkles. "Disgusting!" After making the statement she got out of bed and marched into the bathroom.

We had been lovers for about two years. She was hardly twenty when we met just outside the city on a Sunday afternoon ski trip. All I saw on that day were her eyes and her smile. Everything else was hidden under a baggy but fashionable navy blue ski suit.

But I liked her smile and I loved her eyes. Large, of a clear gray, set wide apart in a face whose high cheekbones betrayed a touch of Slavic blood, it was as if a relay inside me had been tripped by an electric impulse. She realized the effect. From then on I suspected her of having ESP.

We met again the next evening. Without the ski suit. She was beautiful, almost as tall as my own six feet, with a perfect, firm body and a waist two hands could span without difficulty. Her soft light brown hair fell to her shoulders, reflecting the light with each movement of her head. We danced and her body moved with mine as if we had practised for years.

There was no squeamishness. Everything fell into place with a minimum of talk and effort. Maria, in spite of her sophistication and beauty, had never been to bed with a man. But that night she went to bed with me without fuss or drama and without promises. Her relay had been tripped by the same electric impulse as mine.

After Maria had left for the office, I remained in bed for a few more minutes feeling at peace with the world. The pillow beside me smelled of her skin. I basked in the warm glow that filled me. It restored my natural optimism. Everything would be all right. This was a new day. Sanity would prevail.

Sanity hadn't prevailed, although that fact wasn't immediately discernible when I came out into the street. The sun shone brightly in a deep blue sky, the gentle wind, after touching the pine trees of the Vienna

Woods, carried the promise of an early spring. The air was strong and invigorating.

The streets looked as they always had. Nothing had changed. In the bright sunshine, yesterday's fears seemed unreal; they lacked substance.

Albert Sternberg, the editor of Vienna's evening paper *Der Abend,* which used my talent for reporting jobs for which I was paid by the word, was just coming out of the publisher's office. Fat, short, bowlegged, and always good-humored, he never seemed to worry about anything in the three or four years I had known him. I doubted anything could pierce his complacency. His appearance was deceiving, however. He was tough and ruthless when he had to be.

He waddled back to his office and beckoned me to follow him.

"Anything new?" I asked.

"Plenty," he said. "But we can't print it. *Verboten.* If you want to know the score tune in to the German radio. They haven't stopped yakking since yesterday."

"About what? Berchtesgaden?"

"No. That's old stuff. Hitler has put it to Schuschnigg. A full-blown ultimatum. Either we take the Nazis into the government and release all the Nazi punks from jail, or he says he will march into Austria."

"How about Schuschnigg?"

"He isn't saying anything. I'm told he is running up a long-distance telephone bill trying to talk to Paris and London and naturally to Mussolini, his pal."

Schuschnigg had become chancellor when his predecessor, Dollfuss, was assassinated by two Nazis four years earlier. The killers had been hanged but there were hundreds—perhaps even thousands—of the same ilk in the prisons of the country. I shuddered at the thought of what might happen if they were let loose.

"Crazy," I said. "But I don't think Hitler will march.

He's bluffing. He knows France and England won't let him. And Mussolini isn't exactly in love with him either."

France and England had guaranteed Austria's independence. They were pledged to go to war in case of an invasion. Hitler was aware of this. And Mussolini had clearly demonstrated his disapproval of the Hitler-inspired murder of Dollfuss by massing several Italian divisions along the Austrian border to discourage the Fuehrer from following up the assassination with an invasion. All that was historical fact. Every child knew it. France and England wouldn't let Hitler annex Austria; it was inconceivable.

"Silly ass," said Sternberg. "You are a political primitive. The day France and England move a finger to help Austria I'll triple what I pay you now. Mussolini doesn't give a shit either. He kisses Hitler's ass whenever Hitler lets him."

"And him?" I asked, pointing at the publisher's door. "What does he say?"

"He thinks we have had it. He is going away for a while. On a holiday. With Hilda."

Hilda was the old man's secretary. She had the strong, broad-hipped body typical of Austrian peasant stock. It was rumored that the publisher, a man in his sixties, could be aroused only by big, full-breasted women who laughed easily and were not adverse to making love on a desk between dictation. I knew his wife. She was thin, dried up, and probably frigid.

Albert's news punched the first hole in the armor of my confidence. The publisher was known as a clever and cunning operator. And he was courageous. He had guts, and access to information few others had. If he was going on a vacation at a time like this he knew more than we did. But I didn't give up easily. Perhaps it was a genuine vacation. Despite the coincidence, it was possible.

I stayed at the office to do some work but the typewriter keys weren't in their usual places. And my mind kept wandering. I grew progressively more irritated and fed up with myself. Correcting my own mistakes bored me. Disgusted, I finally left.

The gentle breeze of the morning had turned into cold gusts and snowsqualls. The sun was gone, leaving only a thin yellow rim along the horizon. The eery color matched my changed mood.

That night, Maria too failed me. Nature interfered with our plans to make love again. We went to a movie instead: the Marx Brothers with German subtitles. Somehow Groucho wasn't funny that night either. But Maria laughed. I didn't want to spoil her fun so I laughed too.

In the morning Albert phoned. An urgent assignment. Come right away, he said.

I think his telephone call signaled the turning point in my assessment of events which had washed over me so quickly I had been unable to appraise them properly and with reason. I had been floating on a wave of wishful thinking, hoping against hope I would wake up in the morning and everything would be as it was before. It was a convenient delusion. The consequences of Albert's call had a great deal to do with restoring reason to my senses.

Before rushing out I had a quick glance at the morning papers. It was a fait accompli. Schuschnigg had capitulated. The pictures of several prominent Nazis taken into the cabinet were splashed across the front pages. The illegal Nazi party had become legal. The trash and the murderers had been released from the jails.

In the street there was now a difference. Swastika flags had appeared overnight on numerous buildings and now flapped in the breeze. The sight of the red banners with the crooked black cross in the white circle made my blood boil. The faces of the people in the streets irritated me. They too had changed. Most looked depressed. If the Nazis rejoiced, it wasn't visible—at least not yet.

Albert pretended to be his usual cheerful self but he

17

failed to convince me. The stubble of a two-day-old beard gave him a hung over look. Bags under his eyes betrayed a sleepless night.

He was brief and to the point, however. The government had clamped a tight lid on all outside communication. The paper needed to know what was going on in the key areas outside the capital, especially in the western provinces where the Nazis were known to have large pockets of supporters. It was a sensitive assignment but the publisher thought I was the right man for the job. I was to use one of the paper's cars for the trip.

He signed a voucher and handed it to me.

"Get your expense money," he said.

When I was at the door he called out. "Get some German money too," he said, grining all over his moon face, "you might need it sooner than you think."

"Some joke," I said, slamming the door behind me.

I was headed for Innsbruck, the capital of Tyrol, a known Nazi hotseat. Tyrol abuts on Bavaria from whose slums Hitler emerged (which may have had something to do with the high degree of Nazi infestation on our side of the border). It was more tangible than in other parts of the country. At least that was what I thought until I drove into the town of Wels in Upper Austria, population 18,000, some two hundred kilometers west of Vienna.

Twilight was fading into darkness as I drove through the badly lit streets. Everything seemed normal except perhaps for a few more Nazi flags than in other places along the way.

I stopped at an inn on the main square. The town was quiet; there was no one in sight. Shutting off the engine and killing the lights, I leaned over the back of the seat to retrieve my night bag. It took me a minute or so to arrange my things and when I looked up again, the scene had changed. Some twenty or thirty men had

18

slipped from the darkness and were casually standing around the car in a loose semicircle.

In the light of the single bulb over the inn's entrance I saw their rifles. I also saw red armbands with the black swastika in a white circle. I did not like what I saw.

It was only much later that I realized the name of my paper was splashed in capital letters across the body of my red car. *Der Abend* was notoriously anti-Hitler and was hated by every Nazi in the country. The news of my arrival must have preceded me as if I had trekked through the jungle closely monitored by jungle drums. It was the only explanation for the presence of the welcoming committee.

I hesitated for a moment not knowing what to do. I didn't have many alternatives. It was either run or stick it out and try to earn my pay. I decided to earn my pay—against my better judgment.

I got out of the car and said politely, "Excuse me," then pushed in the direction of the inn's entrance. They yielded reluctantly and let me pass. So far so good, I thought. Perhaps they only want to scare me.

The air inside smelled of stale beer and piss. The proprietor, in shirtsleeves, eyed me with suspicion. His belly dipped heavily over the rim of his trousers and the toes pierced the worn slippers. He wasn't sure whether to put me up or throw me out. I could read the dilemma in his face but hoped he would give me a room. I wasn't too anxious to face that crowd outside.

At last he spoke.

"You a Jew?" he asked.

My immediate reaction was to tell him to stick his fucking room up his arse but I thought again of the welcoming committee and checked the impulse. Besides, I tried to convince myself, I was a reporter on assignment. My personal feelings were immaterial. It would make good copy later.

"No," I said, staring straight into his watery eyes. He shrugged and handed me a key.

I took a hasty meal in the small dining room. Some of the jokers who had been outside in the crowd were in a huddle at a table across the room, drinking huge quantities of beer and giving me an occasional glance. Several rifles leaned against the wainscoted wall. The antlered head of a deer looked placidly down on the scene.

When I left the room, all eyes followed me. Bastards, I thought. Savages. Shits!

I think I should say at this point that for a long time I have been suffering from an affliction not listed in any medical encyclopedia, something I call the "five-o'clock syndrome." When it hits me, I wake up at the crack of dawn in agonizing panic, which only fades when I recognize the familiar surroundings of my bedroom. The attack is always triggered by a sound, which could be the footfall on the sidewalk of a pedestrian on his way to the bus stop or the milkman knocking clumsily against the back door.

They always used to come at the crack of dawn. Probably one of the fundamentals drilled into each Gestapo agent or SS man in training. First there was the pounding of heavy boots in the street, stopping abruptly at the door. Then came the pregnant pause. And then the knock at the door.

The knock at dawn.

I trace it back to that night at the inn at Wels. That was where it began. The knock at dawn. The first of many still to come.

It came at the precise moment when dawn straddles the line between night and morning. It tore into my sleep. The room was still dark but the window was already a gray rectangle in the black wall.

The knock came a second time. More impatient this time.

"Who is it?" I mumbled.

"Police," a voice said. "Open up!"

The man in the hall was a policeman in the green uniform of the municipal police. He was flanked by three Nazi storm troopers in brown shirts. Two carried rifles. One, apparently the leader, had an oversized holster hanging from his belt. He was tall and thin.

"Yes?" I asked, looking at the policeman.

"Your identification," he said, adding "please" as an afterthought. He was probably more accustomed to locking up drunks on a Saturday night than fronting for Nazi punks at five in the morning.

In the Austria of the period one didn't argue with the police. Every citizen had been issued with an official identity card which had to be produced on request. That was the law. Contravention was severely punished.

I turned to fetch my wallet. The thin Nazi attempted to follow me but I banged the door shut in his face.

"Dirty Jew!" I heard him mutter through the panel.

Based on centuries-old tradition, official Austrian documents contained the bearer's religious denomination. My identity card was no exception. The officer glanced at it quickly.

"He's no Jew," he told the thin Nazi.

"Shit," said the trooper, ripping the card from the hand of the policeman to make sure he hadn't been fooled by him. Disappointed, he dropped it to the floor. I picked it up.

He and his two goons remained standing there apparently trying to decide on a new course of action. He wasn't very bright. He was confused now that he had lost his trump card. Without a Jew, his position was weak, his prestige threatened. But all was not lost yet. Inspiration struck behind his narrow forehead.

"Shit," he said again. "Maybe he isn't a Jew but he is working for one. Same thing!"

"So?" said the policeman who still didn't like what he

was doing. "What the hell does that mean?"

The Nazi thought that over. Then he shrugged. He didn't know what to do with the discovery.

I ignored him and turned to the officer.

"Anything else?" I asked.

He looked again at the thin man waiting for a cue—which failed to come—and decided to give up.

I skipped breakfast to get out of there as quickly as I could. The owner was already up. I paid and walked out the door. The car was a mess, covered front to back with swastikas and Nazi slogans. "Death to the Jews!" was splashed across the width of the windshield.

The reception committee was on hand again, only much stronger—about fifty, including several women. And no police in sight anywhere.

Well, I thought, this is it as I walked to the car. They made room for me almost politely. I slipped behind the wheel. From the corner of my eye I saw their grinning faces. It was all a big joke. The engine caught quickly and I sighed with relief. They hadn't tampered with the engine. Good, I thought. They want to get rid of me and I was only too glad to oblige. After all, this was still Austria. There were laws. And courts. And retribution. It wasn't the law of the jungle. It was still civilization.

Instinctively, I ducked. A brick came hurtling through the windshield, shattering it into a thousand pieces. A splinter ripped past my cheek. I felt the blood.

Shifting quickly into first gear I leaned on the horn and let it blast, hoping to shock them into giving me enough room to move out. But they didn't budge. Another brick smashed through the rear window. Simultaneously the doors on both sides were yanked open and I was dragged from the car. I tried to fight them off but there were too many of them. Someone tripped me and I fell headlong. I was sure I had cracked my kneecaps.

22

A dozen hands pulled me up and backed me against the wall of the inn. The crowd closed in. The grins were gone, the faces distorted, ugly.

"Kill him!" a woman screamed in the background. "Kill the Jew!" A rock hit my forehead. Blood spurted out, blinding me. My knees buckled.

Now the beasts had tasted blood. They wanted more. They roared. The irrational thought flashed through my mind that Albert would be upset for not getting copy if these animals were to kill me.

And then the unexpected happened. A rescue straight from a Hollywood scenario. Dazed and bleeding, my vision impaired by the blood that streamed down my face and the solid wall of the mob in front, I heard the squeal of tires of a car being braked hard, followed by the sound of an authoritative voice.

"Get back!" barked the voice. "Now! Break it up! On the double!"

The crowd dispersed. They retreated from me. Slowly, loathingly. In their retreat they opened a clearing, which now framed four policemen with carbines and bayonets, led by a civilian. Federal police. Still loyal to the government of yesterday. I had never been so happy at the sight of their gray uniforms before.

I leaned heavily on the civilian as I was led to the car. He turned out to be an inspector. The makeshift bandage he wrapped around my head was soon soaked with blood.

One of his men went for my bag and other things. They were gone, including the portable typewriter.

"Cowards," said the inspector. "Stinking, thieving cowards!"

I was taken to Linz, the capital of the province, and put on a train for Vienna. Before I boarded a doctor came and washed the wound. He also made me swallow a handful of tablets to stop the pain in my head.

At the terminal in Vienna I was just able to make it

to the nearest telephone booth and call Albert. He was annoyed that I was back so soon. The report on my condition made no impression on him.

"Too bad they beat you up," he said. "I was sure it was a good idea but perhaps it wasn't after all. But what the hell—what are you waiting for? Get me the bloody copy. You're wasting my time!"

The world chose the precise moment to start spinning crazily around me. I hung on to the walls of the booth.

"Fuck you!" was all I was able to say as I dropped the receiver. I don't remember how I got home. I only know Maria was there and I slept with my head bedded between her breasts. It didn't ease the pain, but it was heaven.

3

More Trouble

My brother was right. Thirty days, he had said. And he was close. Actually the reprieve had lasted only twenty-eight days when the curtain came down.

It was the night of one of the best dinners Maria had ever cooked. Afterward, the light was low and the radio in the background hummed sweet melodies. Maria's skin smelled of her subtle perfume blended with her own animal scent, which always sent my head spinning.

The music stopped with jarring abruptness. Thinking the dial had slipped I got up to adjust it. Before I touched the knob a voice came through. Schuschnigg's voice. But it wasn't his usual cultured, slightly nasal voice. It was flat, lifeless, devoid of intonation. Tired, disillusioned. He was clearly under stress.

He was brief. He said he had been forced to yield to pressure exerted by Adolph Hitler. The German army was poised at the border. He was turning the government over to Arthur Seyss-Inquart, his minister of the interior and a confirmed Nazi. Schuschnigg, a devout Catholic, ended his message with "May God protect Austria," but his voice faltered. It was as if he realized at that very moment that the court of last resort he was committing his prayer to was either incapable or unwilling to rescue the country from Hitler's grip.

Maria and I sat in silence. Her hand had slipped into mine. I felt her fingers tremble.

Seyss-Inquart was on next. Strangely, he sounded humble, although he had enough reason to sound arrogant. Perhaps he had a premonition his career would be shortlived. In fact, he was hanged as a war criminal less than a decade later. What he said was rubbish. Order must be maintained. It was his duty to protect the country from Jews, Communists, criminals, and other disturbing elements which he failed to identify. Therefore, he said, he had asked the Fuehrer to order the German army into Austria to reestablish law and order. He was still talking when Goering's squadrons flew over the roofs of Vienna, showing how well in advance Hitler had planned the "spontaneous" liberation of Austria.

After Seyss-Inquart had spoken, the station repeated Schuschnigg's message. It was obviously recorded so I turned off the set.

With belated lucidity I now saw how predictable all that had been. I had refused to admit it to myself in spite of my experience at Wels. I should have seen it coming when Schuschnigg, using the breathing spell he had gained by taking the Nazis into his cabinet, had called a national plebiscite for the following Sunday, March 13. He was going to ask the people to make a choice between Hitler and independence. Naturally Hitler considered this a doublecross. The last thing he needed was a plebiscite that might turn against him.

With two days to go until the plebiscite, he told

Schuschnigg to call off the vote or he would send in the tanks. That was Friday afternoon. Schuschnigg realized he was near the end of the line. He was finished whether he buckled under or not. The Wehrmacht would come in any case. So, with nothing to lose, he decided to gamble a little longer. He spent the rest of the day frantically trying to reach Paris, London, and Rome. But it wasn't his lucky day. Paris was without a government. London was in a crisis—Anthony Eden had just resigned as foreign minister to protest Prime Minister Chamberlain's conciliatory attitude toward Hitler. Mussolini had gone on a hunting trip the night before and could not be reached.

Schuschnigg hung on until eight in the evening. When he realized at last that Austria had been sold down the drain, he capitulated, worn down to the bone and hardly able to stand up straight. Many years later, when the Allies liberated the concentration camp in which he had been held, he emerged a white-haired, prematurely aged man.

Maria's head nestled in my chest. She was warm and soft and scared. I kissed her.

"Let's get married," I said, and she nodded in silence. I had no idea what was going to happen but whatever it was I didn't want to lose her. I couldn't stand the thought.

A few days later we slipped from the office for a couple of hours and when we returned, we were man and wife. We didn't tell anyone. I knew the Nazis would come after me sooner or later and I didn't want to cause any trouble for her.

· I left Maria shortly after Seyss-Inquart had gone off the air. The streetcars had stopped running and there were no taxis in sight. I had to walk across the city to get home but decided to drop in at Mother's before going to sleep.

The city had changed in a matter of minutes. The mob

had come out of the woodwork. Hordes of brown-shirted, jack-booted Nazis tramped through the streets, howling, yelling, threatening. They poured into the city core in consecutive waves.

The *Anschluss* was only minutes old but the streets were already littered with the debris of smashed stores owned by Jews or by people known for their anti-Nazi feelings. Looters carted away their booty through gaping doors and shattered windows. Fires flared up in places with the firefighters standing idly by. The mob had slashed the hoses.

People were beaten in the streets for not raising their right arms quickly enough in a salute to the new order. There were dark wet patches on the sidewalk. Blood. The "Night of the Long Knives" the Nazis had promised their opponents all along had finally arrived. The police looked the other way, swastika armlets already pinned to their sleeves. An hour before they had been ardent Austrian patriots.

The narrow streets near Mother's apartment, usually quiet and peaceful, had turned into an anthill. A noisy cluster had formed below her windows. As I approached I couldn't make out what was happening because of the bad light and the unruly mass blocking my view. I began pushing through the crowd and finally, halfway through, I was able to see the spectacle.

Half-a-dozen SA men, some hardly out of their teens, in brand-new brown uniforms, horse whips in hand, were prancing back and forth supervising a small group of people on their knees. Men, women, and children were trying to remove with their bare fingers an anti-Nazi slogan painted on the concrete of the sidewalk. Their nails were broken and their fingers bleeding. An old man with thinning white hair stopped for a moment, exhausted. The whip came down on him with a sickening thud. The mob yelled their approval.

I had elbowed my way to the first line of spectators

when the whip cracked again and a child cried out painfully. An involuntary reflex made me step in the direction of the grinning Nazi but a man beside me grabbed my arm hard.

The Nazi had seen my reaction and came toward me, beckoning at the same time to one of his cohorts to join him.

My neighbor, still holding onto my arm, raised his voice over the din. Instinctively I realized he was doing it for the benefit of the Nazis.

"Take it easy, chum," he yelled. "It's only a bunch of Jews!"

I knew the man. Not by name. I had seen him before in the neighborhood. I knew he was not a Nazi.

For a second I glared into the eyes of the SA man whose hand was firmly around the handle of the whip. The memory of Wels flashed through my mind. I took the cue.

"Oh, Jews," I said casually, "that's different. I couldn't see what was going on in the dark." I forced my face into an apologetic smile.

The tension eased. Their hands were still itching on the whips but they turned back to their victims. I hated myself, knowing there wasn't a thing I could have done. It was futile. Playing the hero would have been suicide and would not have helped the others.

Mother's face was pressed against the windowpane. She was sobbing. My heart was heavy when I saw the fragile, delicate silhouette against the street lights. I put my arm around her and I could smell the familiar fragrance of her hair, still blonde despite her years. The few strands of silver were hardly visible.

"What is going to happen?" she asked.

I didn't answer at once. I was thinking of her bad heart. It had to be done gently.

"I don't know yet," I said, "it all came on so suddenly. Not enough time to think. But it might be a good idea

28

to go away for a while until things settle down. What do you say?"

I had never been able to fool her. I wasn't able to now either.

"It is that bad, is it?" she asked.

I nodded miserably.

"Then you will have to go away, son."

"Yes, probably," I said. "But we will go together. I am not leaving you behind." I didn't tell her about Maria. It could wait.

Her eyes scanned every inch of the room. Very slowly. It was the room where she had been young with father, where her sons had been born and where father had died. The room was part of her and I knew it.

"All right," she said, after a long pause. "I'll be ready when you are."

It had taken only twelve hours for my world to collapse. And yet, as if nothing of consequence had happened, in the morning the sun rose in golden glory in a cloudless, blue sky. Spring was only a week away. The air was mild. Goebbels called it "Hitler weather."

The evening paper had been raided, the machinery, the offices, the presses wrecked and burned. Two type-setters had been killed in the raid and the rest of the staff had disappeared. I was told Albert Sternberg had also been killed and it was probably true. I never heard from him again. The women's weekly, home of my children's column, had been expropriated and was now run by the Nazis. I was out of work.

My brother was out of a job too. The cabaret was boarded up. His telephone rang unanswered and no one answered the door of his flat when I knocked. He was probably holed up somewhere with Fritzi but I knew he would get bored after a few days of seclusion with her. He always did.

The radio had gone berserk. Blaring military marches

and Nazi songs alternated with hour-long speeches by the Fuehrer and some of his stooges, who took over for him when he ran out of voice (which happened from time to time but not often enough). The tanks of the Wehrmacht rumbled through the streets.

People, taken from their beds, began to disappear. Their families were told to keep quiet or they would be arrested too. Urns arrived in the mail with the ashes of the kidnapped people. In some lucky cases, a postcard came with a single preprinted line saying, "I am well," together with the name and the stamp of a concentration camp.

Accepted values changed overnight. It was no longer possible to trust anyone. Brothers turned on brothers, children on their parents. A man was publicly shot for calling Hitler an asshole. He had been denounced by his twelve-year-old son, who was a member of the Hitler Youth.

The firm Maria worked for had been expropriated too. The owner was a Jew. He was shipped to Buchenwald and never heard from again. The firm was taken over by a semi-illiterate night watchman who had been a clandestine Nazi for years.

Jews married to non-Jewish women were arrested, tortured, often castrated and murdered because of *Rassenschande,* the "crime against the purity of the Aryan race," an outcrop of Hitler's sick brain. Ignoring scientific facts, he had proclaimed that an "Aryan" woman suffered irreparable genetic damage when having sexual intercourse with a Jew. The crime called for the death penalty.

But the law of *Rassenschande* was a one-way street. Male "Aryans" were immune to infection by Jewish females. Forty-eight hours after the *Anschluss* there was hardly a Jewess left who had not been raped. Some of the more attractive were assigned to special duty and forced to serve large numbers of men. A girl I had known at university was taken to a building requisitioned as an SA barracks, where she was raped by a whole contingent for three days and nights. On the fourth day she was able to slip away and jumped to her death from the fifth floor.

I tried to get in touch with several foreign correspondents I had befriended. Most had been expelled. Telephone and telegraph lines had been cut. Austria was shut off from the rest of the world.

Hitler arrived in Austria with medieval pomp, followed by Goering and Goebbels a few days later. Each visit was a pretext for a new purge. Normal life had come to a standstill. The days turned into nightmares and the nights into deadly traps. A knock at dawn meant the Gestapo and the end.

4

Closing In

In the midst of the chaos my brother emerged from seclusion. He said he had come to the conclusion that the whole schizophrenic affair couldn't last. It was irrational. It bore the symptoms of an early death. He wasn't going to leave. Vienna was his life. He was going to stay.

I agreed with him that the Nazi takeover was too unreal to last. It was doomed. But doomed or not, the trick was to stay alive while it lasted. The debate took place in the back room of a small café I used for headquarters, since the streets had become unsafe.

We were joined by Kurt, a close childhood friend. He and I used to steal apples from the corner grocer on our way to school.

Kurt came from a family of professionals but there was also a sprinkling of priests if I remember correctly.

Incongruously, he looked like a Jew. Whether this was due to a genetic freak or to an indiscretion by one of his ancestors remained an unanswered question. He had been kidded for it for as long as I knew him but under the present circumstances his prominent nose and fiery red hair could hardly be considered an asset.

Kurt was deeply disturbed. The girl he intended to marry had been raped the previous night by two uniformed Nazis and left dazed and bleeding at a deserted spot near the Danube. The police shrugged it off. They said they had no jurisdiction over the Nazis.

Kurt was still talking when the door swung open and two SS men walked in. Big and husky and over six feet tall, they stood there in their black uniforms, blackjacks in their hands, unhurriedly taking in the scene.

"Cozy," said one of them, sneering. His accent was Prussian. "Get up, swine!" he yelled.

We jumped to our feet.

He looked us over. Slowly. Arrogantly. He was grinning now. "Haven't you swine forgotten something?" he asked, with deceiving softness in his voice.

Our arms went up. "Heil Hitler!"

"Much better," he said. "You are learning."

He turned to Kurt. "You here!"

Kurt ticked to attention.

"Jew?"

"No," said Kurt unhappily, fully aware of his long-standing handicap.

"Liar," said the Nazi, and with the deft motion of a cat he cleared the space that separated him from Kurt. The half-circle described by the blackjack as it swished through the air became a blurred arc. Kurt slumped to the floor, a thin trickle of blood oozing from the corner of his mouth. The other Nazi, without wasting a second, grabbed his legs and dragged him out through the door. The speed and coordination of the two men betrayed long practice.

The butcher was still in the same spot, his booted legs wide apart, arms akimbo. Now he concentrated on me, looking pensively at my blond hair, obviously trying to decide what to do with me.

"Keeping company with dirty Jews," he said. Then he spat in my face. I felt the saliva running down my skin and the blood shot up into my head in sudden fury. I clenched my fists. He saw the reflex. It pleased him. It was just what he wanted.

"Nasty," he said.

He hit me with the back of his hand across the mouth and he was as strong as a prize bull. I reeled over backward, taking the table with me. I heard the sound of cracking wood before blacking out.

When I came to, the Nazis were gone. My brother stopped slapping my face with a wet towel. My lips were cut and my teeth hurt. Kurt was gone too. I never saw him again.

Although we were both badly shaken, the incident failed to make a dent in my brother's mental stance. "Isolated episode," he ruled with grating superiority, "power-drunk punk having a private ball. Sadistic moron. Doesn't mean a thing in the overall picture."

The next day brought me another shock. I ran into Felix. I thought I was seeing a ghost. Him, of all people. Felix was a cousin. A prominent socialist, former member of parliament, doctor of Philosophy, author, and generally considered future party leader despite his relative youth. He was only forty. His anti-Nazi record was well established.

"Are you mad?" I asked as soon as the shock had worn off. "Are you still here?"

He looked at the bruises on my face but made no comment. He just shrugged.

"I went into exile once," he said. "That was enough for one lifetime. This time I stay."

He fled to Czechoslovakia after Dollfuss had smashed

Austrian democracy in 1934 with the few pieces of artillery the army was permitted to keep after the First World War. Later, after the Nazis assassinated Dollfuss, Schuschnigg pardoned the political exiles and Felix came back, although not to parliament. All this may sound confusing, unless it is remembered that life in the Vienna of the period wasn't the kind that inspired Johann Strauss to write his operetta "Die Fledermaus."

"You are insane," I said. "This is suicide. They'll kill you as sure as the Amen in a prayer."

He shrugged again. "I'll take the chance," he said and smiled. The thought streaked through my mind that he was just as crazy as my brother. It seemed to run in the family. Perhaps I would be the next to flip. The notion frightened me.

Felix hadn't been back to his apartment since the night of the *Anschluss*. There was no need to make it easy for the Gestapo. I took him home and gave him my bed for the night. In the morning he left and that was the last time I saw him. He died in 1942 in the concentration camp of Dachau.

The backhand the SS man had given me produced at least one beneficial effect. It brought home to me the realization it was high time to get out of Austria. But there was one hitch: I was broke. In the Austria of the thirties one did not save money. The memory of postwar inflation, coupled with the 1929 crash was still fresh. Besides, I had always spent my money as quickly as it came in. I didn't even have enough for the train to the border.

But luck was with me. My problem was solved the very next day by Eric, a fashionable photographer who specialized in pictures of nude women whose poses straddled the laws of pornography. He was much in demand by magazines for men.

When I met him he was wearing the oversized swastika badge only Nazi party members of long standing were allowed to wear and Eric was definitely not a Nazi. His father taught Hebrew at a Jewish seminary and his mother was the daughter of a cantor, a Jewish temple singer. It was most disturbing.

"Christ," was all I managed to say, "have you gone raving mad too?"

"Not really," he said. "It's a good disguise. They don't bother me when I wear it. I look like one of them."

"They'll crucify you when they catch you."

"So what," he said. "What's the difference? The fucking bastards will crucify me anyway whether I wear this or not. I am a Jew. Remember? An outcast. I have no illusions. They picked up my father. He is sixty-seven. He has never hurt a fly. I don't know what they did with him. Nobody knows. He is probably dead by now. My brothers are holed up somewhere. My sister is hiding in an attic. She is afraid they will rape her and they probably will too."

I knew his sister. A tall, willowy girl with long black hair which she often wore in a bun. Quite beautiful. He was right. They would.

"I don't want to talk about it or I'd go nuts," he said. "But how about you? Are you going to hang around till they grab you by the balls? I think you're even nuttier than me."

I told him I had to find money first.

"How much do you need?" he asked.

I told him.

"No problem. It's easy. I can get it for you. But I can't do it alone. You've got to help me get it."

He began to explain, and the more he explained the crazier it sounded. Then, on second thought, his story fitted straight into the whole schizophrenic scenario. His studio had been ransacked and his equipment stolen, he said, and afterward he was able to get himself a phony identity card which he used to apply for a job as a solicitor for the *Stuermer*, Julius Streicher's filthy newspaper which advocated the eradication by brute force of the Jewish race. He sold subscriptions door-to-door. The commission was generous.

My face must have shown what I thought.

"Don't be an asshole too," he said. "Don't be stupid. Don't feel sorry for the bastards. You saw them the day Hitler came; how they yelled in the streets, screaming, howling, and killing Jews. It was great. But that was a couple of months ago. By now they've sobered up, the stinking cowards. They see what's going on. They are scared. So they buy insurance. They buy the fucking newspaper to prove they are good Nazis. They come up with the money even before I have finished my spiel. I have no compunction. I like it. I love it! I love their money. I need it. I want to scram too!"

I could see his logic. What I couldn't see was how I fitted into the thing. I certainly wasn't going to sell the *Stuermer* door-to-door, and I said so.

No need, said Eric. His plan was simple. Julius Streicher was going to finance our escape. It was his money we were going to take but it could only be done on a Sunday night. On the weekends the receipts were always big because most of the prospective victims were at home from work, easy prey for the salesmen. Money rolled in. The solicitors dropped off their collections at the end of the day at a central office in the third district of the city where it was locked up overnight. According to Eric the safe was old and the combination old-fashioned. Eric had duplicate keys to the office. He said he knew all about safes and that it was a cinch to open this one. But he needed a helper. A lookout. He would split the take with me.

It was Nazi money. I had no compunction either.

Two days later we were waiting in the street and did so until the lights went out on the second floor of the building. Several people left, locking the massive front door behind them. We gave it another fifteen minutes. Then Eric unlocked the door and disappeared inside. In case of trouble I was to throw a raw egg against the window. It was Eric's idea. I had half a dozen in my pocket in case I missed.

Waiting was boring. The street remained deserted except for a few pedestrians who showed no interest. At last, the window upstairs opened and Eric whistled softly. I crossed the street.

"Come up," he whispered.

In the beam of the flashlight the safe was wide open. Beside it were three bulging briefcases. I picked up two, closed them with some difficulty, and followed Eric down the stairs.

The foot of the stairs was about thirty or forty feet away from the street door and we had almost made it when the huge door suddenly swung open. Eric grabbed me and we stopped.

The hall was dark but in the light filtering in from the street I saw the silhouette of a young woman. Shit, I thought. Trouble. Why in hell now? At the last moment!

She was as startled as we were but when she pushed the door open wider, the light fell on Eric's face.

"Why, Eric!" she exclaimed, surprised and apparently impressed by his badge. She followed up with a resounding "Heil Hitler!"

"Heil Hitler!" crowed Eric in turn. The relief in his voice was unmistakable. "Helga," he said, "how nice. I thought you had left town. I am so glad to see you. Where have you been?"

He laid it on thick. Taking a quick step forward, he kissed her for a long time and gradually her hands went up along his back and up to his neck. I knew he was putting on an act. He had no other choice. But there we were with three bulging briefcases full of stolen money. There were two million people living in Vienna at the time and we had to pick the one person who knew Eric and could identify him. I nearly cried in frustration.

But Eric was still kissing her. He seemed to be enjoying it.

"What are you doing here?" he asked between kisses.

"I live here," she said. "On the third floor."

"Alone?"

"No. With my brother." There must have been a cloud of disappointment on Eric's face. She saw it and added quickly, "But he isn't here. He is away. In training. He is in the SS."

Eric clutched her a little closer when he turned to me.

"Sorry, pal," he said apologetically, "something just came up. I'll be delayed for a while. Why don't you go ahead in the meantime. I'll see you later at your place."

He showed up shortly before daybreak.

"Everything's under control," he said. "She doesn't know you."

"Good," I said, "but she sure knows you."

"No problem. She thinks I'm a good Nazi. She also liked the way I fucked her. I tell you, I was really good. Four times. I didn't know I still had it in me. She's a good piece. And she loved every minute of it. She'll shut up."

"Rassenschande," I said, "on top of breaking and entering."

"Screw Rassenschande," he said. "I have it in for that asshole Hitler. A load of good Jewish sperm in an Aryan cunt will do the Nordic race a hell of a lot of good. Who knows, it could even be the next Fuehrer." The thought amused him.

"They'll cut your balls off."

"Too late. I'm off for the Hungarian border within the hour. It's all arranged."

We divided the loot. It was more than I had expected.

38

He scanned the street from behind the drapes to make sure the house wasn't being watched and then quickly left.

I was still biding my time, probably because of the insane subconscious hope for an unexpected change in the political situation. Fortunately Bruno put a brusque end to my inertia. He saved my life.

I didn't recognize him when I passed him in the street. When I did I didn't trust my eyes. He was in the black uniform of the SS but the silver trimmings indicated rank. He was an officer. Even in a world in which all accepted values had gone topsy-turvy this was deeply disturbing.

Bruno and I had been friends for years. Politically, he had always been sort of a mystery to me although we were rather close, even to the extent of occasionally sharing the same girl on one of our frequent skiing trips into the mountains. I knew he had been in Moscow for a year or so claiming to study the language but that was all I knew. Seeing him now in the uniform of Hitler's hated élite guard, my heart skipped a beat.

He had seen me before I recognized him. Automatically I veered toward him but I saw his eyebrows go up in a silent signal. I caught on and passed him without a sign of recognition.

I stopped, feigning interest in a store window, watching his reflection in the glass. He entered a small bar at the end of the block. I found him in the washroom.

He was furious.

"You stupid sonofabitch," he hissed. "You brainless moron. Don't you know the bastards are on to you. They're watching you. Don't you know they got Felix?"

"Through me?" I asked stupidly.

"Through you, you idiot!"

Christ, I thought. Felix! They used me as bait. And all the time I thought I was lucky they weren't interested in me. How idiotic of me. I was bait. I was to lead them to the others. They were playing cat and mouse with me. My mind was in turmoil. Sweat broke out in my armpits. In my confusion I was able to formulate one question which I knew was stupid.

"How come you are SS?"

"Idiot," he said again. "I thought you had more brains. It's my job. Undercover."

For a moment I felt good. Bruno was still Bruno. At least one solid point in the dizzy merry-go-round.

"They'll kill you," I said suddenly, realizing I was getting redundant. I had said the same thing to several people in the last few days.

"They won't," he grinned. "I can handle that. But you are a pain in the ass. You've got to get out—and fast!"

"I know. But it isn't easy. The borders are watched."

"Go over the mountains. Most do."

"No dice. I'm taking Mother. I can't leave her here."

He gave me a thoughtful look. He liked Mother and the apple strudel she baked so well. He never knew his own mother. He had been raised in an orphanage.

"Got your passport?" he asked.

I nodded.

"Don't use it. They have you pegged. You have to get one in a different name. Got any money?"

"Some."

"Three thousand?"

I nodded again.

He tore a piece of toilet paper off the roll on the wall and scribbled an address on it.

"Go there. Don't put it off. They'll fix you up. Tell them you are ready for the resurrection. Got that? Ready for the resurrection? Give them passport pictures and the money. And for Christ's sake don't stall!" He squeezed my shoulder. "Good luck you stupid sonofabitch," he said, opening the door a tiny crack to peer outside. Everything seemed clear. He turned back to me.

"Call me tomorrow night at eight. At the old number. I want to know how you made out."

He opened the door again and slipped out. "Make sure you aren't followed or you *are* dead," he said, before closing the door behind him.

I gave him a headstart of several minutes and left.

5
Under the Wire

The address was that of a small shoemaker shop in a working man's district. The air smelled of leather. The small man behind the counter, busy with a boot, looked at me over the rim of his glasses. He had wary eyes.

I felt foolish reciting that I was ready for the resurrection and expected him to say "Amen," but he told me to give him the pictures and to sit down. He disappeared in the back after locking the door and hanging out a sign that read "Back in five minutes."

After a little more than an hour he returned and handed me three passports. They looked authentic, as did the Swiss entry and Nazi exit visas, complete with the official Nazi seal showing an eagle with extended wings, the talons clutching a swastika.

The little man told me to sign my new name on the blank space under my picture. It gave me a funny feeling. Our family name was now Winkler, not Martin anymore. We would have to get used to it.

Maria was waiting for me in a side street in the small café we used for our fleeting get-togethers. I gave her the new passport and explained the plan. Mother and I were taking the night train to Zurich on the following evening. As soon as I was safely across the border I would send her a postcard saying simply that I was having a wonderful time. After establishing a base in Switzerland I would write again. We agreed on an uncomplicated code, a series of successive cards, each containing one key word. The sum of the key words was to give her the information needed to follow me.

She understood I had to get out first and without her. If they caught me on the train in her company she would be in trouble too. It was senseless to endanger her as well. She saw the logic but didn't like the idea of being left behind. I kissed her once more in the doorway. She didn't cry. Her back was straight as she marched down the street like a soldier going to war. I watched her as long as I could.

Bruno had said they were on to me and the thought of the phony passports in my pocket made me uneasy. The logical thing was to get out of circulation to minimize the chances of being picked up in the street. I knew what I was going to do. I was going to spend the night at Mother's. It was unlikely they would watch her place too unless they considered a fragile old woman a threat to the Third Reich. But first I had to grab what I needed for the trip. I wasn't going back to the apartment afterwards.

I quickly packed. I wanted to travel lightly but in the last moment I threw in almost a dozen of my favorite books I thought I couldn't do without and which made the suitcase heavier than I had intended. But what the hell, I thought, the weight won't kill me. It's just an overnight trip.

The suitcase was heavy. I took to the side streets and zigzagged to Mother's apartment, looking over my shoulder from time to time to make sure I wasn't being followed. It was getting dark. At eight I lifted the receiver to dial Bruno but something made me stop halfway. I don't know what it was. Premonition, apprehension, a hunch—I haven't the faintest idea. I thought I was getting jittery and put the phone closer to my ear.

At first I couldn't detect anything out of the ordinary. The usual hum was there. But there was also something else, something intangible. All of a sudden I knew what it was. The hum. It had changed. The pitch was different. Something had been done to the phone. I listened again and then I heard it. The faint and unmistakable sound of breathing.

I hung up, bathed in a sudden sweat. Things were closing in faster than I had expected. I felt trapped. I peered through a crack between the curtains. The street was empty except for a lonely figure who looked familiar. It was Bruno in civilian clothes. He was standing at the corner across the street from where he could keep an eye on both approaches to the house. Occasionally he glanced up in the direction of the window. Something unexpected must have come up or Bruno wouldn't be taking such a chance. I was sure I hadn't told him I was going to be here. If he knew I was here, the others knew it too. Fear swamped me again, cold, irrational fear.

It was obvious he was here because he wanted to tell me something. I went downstairs and out into the street. He followed me to the tobacconist at the corner. I asked for a pack of cigarettes; he bought a newspaper which he noisily unfolded.

"You've got to get out," he said over the rustle of the paper. "Right away! Now! They are coming for you in the morning. Drop everything. There is a train in an hour. You can just make it. Gives you a jump of eight hours on them. Get going! Move your ass!"

"I've got to tell Maria," I said.

"I'll tell her. Your phone is tapped. Now scram!"

My brother was at Mother's place. Fortunately she was already packed and needed only a few minutes for the finishing touches. I took her two suitcases and my brother picked up mine.

"Holy smoke," he said, "that's a heavy brute. What

have you got in there? Rocks?"

A taxi was out of the question. It could be traced too easily. The streetcar was painfully slow but managed to drop us at the station with ten minutes to spare.

When the train pulled out I caught a final glimpse of my brother. I'll never forget his expression. I am sure he realized his fatal mistake at the last minute. Why I didn't drag him bodily with me I'll never know. The remorse is still bitter after all these years.

The train was scheduled to reach the Swiss border around eight in the morning. For a while we shared the compartment with several people but gradually they disappeared after a few stops. We were left alone. Around midnight we stretched out on the two benches. I covered Mother with my coat. She slept, or pretended to sleep. I couldn't. Prone on my back, arms crossed behind my head, I was listening to the clacking of the wheels.

I was scared again. So far I had been lucky, but Bruno's remark stuck in my mind. "Gives you a jump of eight hours on them," he had said. Eight hours. The more I thought about those eight hours the more scared I became. Eight hours wasn't enough. It was a simple problem of arithmetic. The train was due at the border at eight. If they came looking for me back home at five in the morning as it was Gestapo practice, they had three hours to wonder why I hadn't waited for them. The inevitable delay for passport inspection at the border would easily give them another hour or two, altogether four, perhaps even five. Time enough to get on the phone and alert all border points. And I was helpless. Trapped on the train. I had a sudden urge to get off and try my luck on foot but I couldn't do it because of Mother. The tension tied my guts into solid knots.

But just when my spirits sagged to a new low I remembered my brand-new identity. Idiot, I thought, you have nothing to fear. You are Frederick Winkler now.

They wouldn't be looking for you—unless they had a good description, in which case I was sunk. Damn it, I thought, it's hopeless. A vicious circle. Luckily exhaustion caught up with me and I fell asleep.

When I woke up it was morning. Mother and I had an early breakfast in the dining car. The load on my nerves seemed to get heavier with each passing kilometer. According to my calculation the eight-hour reprieve had run out three hours earlier. By now they knew full well I had slipped through the mesh. The next hour was critical. I was right in the middle of the danger zone. Every fiber in my body was aware of it. I forced myself not to show any fear. Fear arouses suspicion. I remembered the Edgar Allan Poe story of the man who had hidden his murdered wife's body under the floorboards, No one suspected him, but it was fear that finally gave him away. I couldn't let it happen to me.

The train pulled into the pleasant border station. Feldkirch. The platform was crowded with steel-helmeted soldiers. The odd brown-shirt. A group of civilians. Official-looking. Gestapo most likely. I had the chilling thought that the next few minutes would decide whether I was going to live or die. The culmination point was almost reached. The watershed. Strangely, at that very moment the chill left me and I grew very calm. I knew the uncertainty would be over in a short time. The end of intolerable suspense. It was either deliverance or the end. In that same instant I became very lucid. All fear was gone. I think it was due to some sort of chemical reaction that affected my brain. Probably a massive shot of adrenalin somehow released into my bloodstream by a protective mechanism. All of a sudden I felt elated. Let them come, the fucking, no-good bastards!

Our car was one of the first behind the steel back of the electric locomotive. It was a long train. The engine had run a good five-hundred feet beyond the edge of the platform. We finally stopped. I lowered the window and leaned out. The cluster of civilians was breaking up. They boarded the cars in pairs. Passport inspection.

Waiting chewed on my nerves again. At last they came to our compartment.

"Passport control," said the shorter of the two. I was nearest to the door and he looked at me.

"Your name?"

"Winkler," I said, "Frederick Winkler." The unfamiliar name sounded hollow to my ears.

He looked at a sheet in his hand. Probably a list of names. I couldn't help wondering whether my real name was on it. Most likely. But the name Winkler wasn't because he looked up at me again.

"Passport."

I handed him both passports.

He scrutinized each page with great care, making notes on a small pad as he went along. The tension was again unbearable. I felt sweat pouring down my chest and back under my shirt, convinced he could hear the drumbeat of my heart. I thought of Edgar Allan Poe again.

He stopped writing. "Reason of trip?" he asked.

I had expected the question. "Health," I said. "Mother has a bad heart. I am taking her to relatives in Switzerland for a rest."

His expression was bland. I wished I had thought of getting something signed by a doctor. Too late now. I decided to make the story more plausible at the risk of overplaying it.

"I am not staying with her," I said. "I am coming back."

Whether he believed me or not I don't know. He wasn't quite ready to accept the story but my casual manner may have fooled him. He had no idea how hard it was to sound casual. I know it was touch and go because it was with visible reluctance that he finally put a stamp under the German exit visa, tossed the passports back at me, and stomped out of the compartment.

I looked at Mother. Her face was ashen and she was trembling.

The Swiss Immigration man came, a friendly, fat man with a round red face and a handlebar mustache. He was making sure we hadn't anything to declare. Now it was his turn to stamp the passports.

The minutes dragged on. Nothing happened. Tension built up again. What was holding them up? Why weren't we moving? Every minute increased the chance of detection. My nerves felt like ropes under my skin.

At last there was a whistle and a second later a jerking wave ran through the whole length of the train. We began to move. I exhaled with relief, realizing I had been holding my breath for an uncomfortably long spell.

I lowered the window again and looked back. The two Gestapo men were still standing on the platform watching the train pull out. Good riddance, I thought. To hell with you!

I was about to pull back from the window when a commotion erupted back at the platform. Someone came storming out of the station waving a piece of paper. The short Gestapo man ripped it from his hand. He took a quick glance at it and yelled at the conductor to stop the train but the man didn't hear him or didn't want to. The train kept on moving.

The stocky man leaped forward. The last car was just passing him and he began to run alongside, rapidly approaching the end of the platform where the pavement stopped and the ground fell away by several feet. I hoped he wouldn't see the drop and break his fat neck. At the last moment he jumped and cleared the abyss that had suddenly opened before him, landing precariously on the running board.

My instinct told me what had happened. They had

transmitted my description. I was right. Just a few minutes passed before the compartment door was pushed open violently. The man's breath came in short gasps.

"You," he bellowed, pointing at me, "you come with me—and no funny tricks!"

Mother shivered and stirred but I held her back patting her hand. I needed time to think.

"Get up!" he yelled, having recouped some of his breath. "Didn't you hear me?"

"I did," I said, trying to sound surprised. "But why?"

"Don't play the idiot. Get up! For the last time!"

"I don't understand," I said innocently. "Are you a policeman?"

"Geheime Staatspolizei," he said, flipping up his lapel exposing a badge of shiny brass. "Gestapo. Are you coming now or not?"

I needed more time. The station we had just left was close to the border. How close I didn't know, nor did I know whether or not we had crossed the border in the meantime. The train was laboring up the mountain and wasn't going very fast. For all I knew we could still be in Nazi territory but if I could hold out long enough I might be able to bluff my way out. I had to stall. He had no power on the other side of the border and he knew it. Yet there was still one more catch. There could still be another stop at the border proper. There could be soldiers, more Gestapo, a final check, a last control. The Germans were a thorough breed. In that case the game was up but I couldn't take that for granted. I had to risk it. There was no other way short of strangling him, so I played dumb.

"State Police?" I said, putting as much surprise into my voice as I was capable of. "I really don't understand. German State Police did you say?"

"Gestapo," he confirmed. "Now get going!" His face had turned purple. He was rapidly approaching the end of his patience. The explosion was near. He was probably thinking of the complications if he tried to arrest me once the train was on Swiss territory.

"I don't think I will," I said. "I think you are making a mistake. I haven't done anything. Besides, we are not in Germany any longer. You have no rights here even if you are Gestapo."

"Shut up!" he yelled. "This is a German train. You are under arrest!"

"Under arrest? But why?"

"Never mind why!" His voice was cracking. "Get the hell going you stinking swine before I drag you out of here by your scrawny neck! Get up! For the last time!"

I didn't move. A sign flashed across the window. One word: Liechtenstein. We had crossed the border. There hadn't been a last minute stop after all. The tension was gone. It was a good time for an obscenity, I suddenly felt.

"Fuck you, you bastard," I said pleasantly. "You've missed the boat."

He made a step forward, murder in his eyes. He had seen the sign too. I stood up. I was more than a foot taller than him and he hadn't expected that. Instantly he reached into his pocket and came out with a gun. A thirty-eight. A deadly weapon at close range.

Mother cried out but I patted her head.

"All right," I said, trying to look disheartened. "You don't have to shoot. I'm coming."

He wasn't convinced but stepped back to make room for me, watching me closely. I reached up to the luggage rack.

He yelled again. "What are you doing?"

"Getting my suitcase," I said. "I need a few things."

He said nothing but followed every move I made.

It was a solid suitcase—pigskin with heavy brass corners for reinforcement. Made to last a lifetime. With the books I had packed it weighed at least sixty or seventy pounds. I feigned difficulty dislodging it from the rest of the luggage and put my right foot up on the bench, grabbing the handle with one hand and easing it out with the other. The maneuver wasn't easy and he watched me like a hawk, the gun pointed directly at me. I knew he would shoot at the first suspicious move. I tried not to make one.

The case came free. He was about four feet away and the foot on the bench gave me the leverage I needed. I yanked the suitcase from its perch and sent seventy pounds of solid pigskin straight into his face. It came in at a sharp angle, the brass edge tearing into his right eye with the force of a bullet.

He screamed. The impact propelled him backward and he crashed into the wall, slumping to the floor almost in slow motion. The gun clattered across the boards. He howled again. A mixture of blood and a whitish fluid oozed from under the hand he had pressed against the spot where his eye had been. For a moment I felt sorry for him but only for a moment. He would have killed me without hesitation and probably bragged about it later over a mug of beer.

Then unexpectedly the train slowed again and for a second the knot of fear in the pit of my stomach returned. Was it because of me? If so, I might as well use his gun on myself.

But it was only a whistle stop. The train continued on. I knew I had to work fast. He was heavy but I dragged him by his legs to the outer platform of the car. Stunned and only half-conscious, he did not resist. He wasn't howling anymore but whimpering in a high pitch while pressing his hands over his face.

I opened the exit door and hauled him to the edge of the steps. The train gave a sudden lurch which helped me to heave him out. He bounced off the steps and tumbled down the embankment. My foot touched the gun. I threw it after him.

When I returned, Mother didn't say a word but she was as white as a ghost.

The conductor rushed into the compartment.

"What's going on here?" he asked nervously.

"Nothing," I said. "My mother isn't feeling well. That's all."

He looked at Mother's face. "Yes, I can see that. But that man who jumped out . . .?"

"What about him? He was in a hurry. Almost missed his stop."

The conductor gave me a long look. I ignored him and sat down beside Mother. He shrugged and disappeared into the corridor.

The whistle gave out with a triumphant blast as the train rolled into Switzerland.

6

The Black Mercedes

My first act on Swiss soil was to flush the phony passports down the toilet at the railway station in Zurich, after having ripped them into a hundred tiny pieces. With the genuine passports which had traveled with us hidden inside the lining of one of the suitcases, I registered at a small hotel for the night. In the morning I found two furnished rooms near the lake.

My second act was to send half-a-dozen postcards to Maria with the coded message to drop everything and come.

I used the next few days to make contact with several journalists I had met in my newspaper work. It paid off. A news agency asked me to write an eyewitness piece on the "Night of the Long Knives." Later they wanted more human interest material and let me use an old Underwood typewriter in their office. The money they paid me assured us of food for a few more weeks, which was good because my German money was useless. No one in Switzerland wanted any part of Hitler's German marks.

Maria finally arrived from Vienna. A telegram had preceded her. This time her eyes were moist when she stepped from the train and she couldn't speak for several minutes. Although she couldn't have known about the episode on the train, she had guessed there had been trouble because the day after my escape all hell had broken loose. My apartment had been sealed off, as had Mother's. SS guards were posted in both places. They had looked for my brother too, probably to use him to blackmail me into coming back, but he had gone into hiding and had slipped a note to Maria before she left. He was all right, the note said. He was going to stick it out and not to worry about him.

I took Maria home. The bed was wide enough for both of us and we consummated our marriage as soon as Mother had gone to her room. Our honeymoon had begun at last.

It lasted exactly twenty-four hours. Then a uniformed policeman came and handed me a summons addressed to Paul Martin to appear within the hour before a Commissioner Schmidt, in charge of aliens. At the same time the postman handed me a registered letter. The envelope bore the eagle and swastika of the Third Reich. It came from the German consul. He too wanted to see me. Right away! I knew I had to see the commissioner but I had no desire to see the Nazi consul. The fact he knew where I lived was disturbing enough.

The commissioner's office was one of Spartan simplicity. Sunlight streamed through the open window. The top of his desk was empty except for a thin file folder with my name on it. It was upside down but I had no trouble reading it, since it was written in capitals two inches high.

Tall, in his sixties, with a broad and clean forehead, the commissioner didn't believe in nonessential talk. He came straight to the point.

"We have no record of an entry visa issued to a Paul Martin," he said. "Will you explain how you entered Switzerland?"

It was a question I had been afraid of from the beginning. I had come on a forged passport with a forged visa. This was a serious offense. I could be jailed and deported. The German border was just a few kilometers away. I shuddered at the thought. The commissioner was waiting for my answer. He did not look like a man I could easily fool—which was not my intention anyway. He looked like an honest and intelligent man. It was best to take a chance and tell him the truth.

I unraveled the whole skein, for obvious reasons skipping only the incident on the train and he didn't interrupt once. Afterward, he said nothing for several minutes. When he finally spoke, my optimism warmed up again. His voice was still clipped and official, but I thought I detected a slightly warmer tinge to it.

"To sum it up," he said, "you used forgery to gain admission into Switzerland."

I nodded.

"This is grounds for deportation. You know that, don't you?"

"Yes," I said. "But there are extenuating circumstances. I am a political refugee. I am asking for asylum."

"Out of the question," he said.

"But why?"

He shrank back into silence, his gaze fixed at the wall behind me.

"We are expecting a request from the German ambassador for your extradition," he said.

"But I am not a German," I said heatedly. "I am Austrian. Switzerland has not acknowledged the annexation of Austria. He has no bloody right!"

My outburst amused him. A faint smile crossed his lean face.

"Maybe so," he said. "Maybe he has no political justification. But you are forgetting a minor detail."

He saw the question in my eyes.

"They don't want you for anything political. They want you for attempted murder of a German police officer."

Attempted murder! So that's how they played the game? Very clever. They knew the Swiss wouldn't extradite a political refugee. That wasn't done in Switzerland. Lenin had been an exile in Switzerland and thousands before and after him. The Nazis knew that. But attempted murder wasn't political. It was criminal. This way the Swiss could not refuse the German request.

No wonder the Swiss authorities were concerned, which was the reason for the hasty summons. It wasn't a matter of a phony passport. The Swiss wouldn't have bothered. Not in the light of the happenings next door. Each week hundreds of hapless refugees came straggling through the snow and the ice of the mountains, some without papers, others with documents as phony as mine. They were all given asylum—temporarily at least.

The commissioner read my thoughts.

"It's a tricky situation," he said. "They claim you tried to kill a German policeman. You can't prove you didn't. We have to take their word for it. It's a criminal offense. It isn't political. We have a mutual treaty with them for the extradition of criminals. We can't say no. Do you understand? We can't antagonize them. They have eleven divisions at the border. We are a people of four million; they are seventy millions. We can't afford to provoke them."

He let it sink in.

"I know what happened on the train, although you preferred not to tell me. It was reported to me the same day. I also know you were in a tough spot and in your shoes I would probably have done what you did. But there isn't a thing I can do."

"Am I under arrest?"

He shook his head.

"No, not yet. So far it isn't official but I was told the papers will be here in a day or two. When they come my hands will be tied."

My mind was racing ahead again. If it is still unofficial why was he tipping me off? There was only one possible explanation: he wanted to help me. He was no friend of Hitler's.

"I need more time," I said. "Two days is not enough. I can't just grab my wife and mother and run. I need at least a week."

He thought this over and a faint smile softened his features momentarily. He was trying to think of a way. The idea of putting something over on the Nazis seemed to delight him.

"I can possibly stall it for a week," he said after a while, "but not much longer. I am going to request verification of the charge. In any case it is my duty in an extradition case involving a fugitive from justice who has not been convicted by a legitimate court of law. That will take a week."

"A week is all I need," I said, my whole body sagging with relief.

I handed him the consul's letter. He read it and frowned. "I don't like what it implies," he said. "It means they don't trust us and are playing both ends. They are making sure they'll get you one way or the other. Be careful."

"What can they do?" I said. "This is Switzerland. I'm outside their reach."

"I wonder," he said pensively. "People have disappeared before. Dragged back across the border. We can't prove it but we know. As I said, be careful. Damned careful."

He saw me out. I was halfway down the stairs when I heard him say "Watch your step." My mind was preoccupied as I came out into the street. I crossed to the other side barely aware of a black Mercedes parked at the curb. It was a large touring car, its canvas top up and the side flaps tightly closed. I thought it a bit silly to have the top up on such a warm sunny day. The inside would be a steam bath. Crazy!

I hit on the idea of canvassing some of the journalists at the agency for a suggestion on how to get out of the fix. I certainly didn't have a clue. Also, I still had some money coming which I thought I would pick up before breaking the news to my small harem. This new twist bothered me, of course, but strangely there was something else that tugged on my mind. For some unaccountable reason I felt a peculiar uneasiness. I had no explanation for the feeling until I looked back and saw the black Mercedes again. It was moving slowly toward the intersection where I was standing.

All of a sudden I knew what was disturbing me. The car! I had seen it before. Several times in fact but hadn't paid much attention. Mercedes were all over the place. It was one of the most popular makes.

The black car passed by me slowly. Neither the driver nor the passenger beside him seemed to notice me, which made me think perhaps my imagination was working overtime again. Nerves.

At the news agency I talked to several of the newsmen and we kicked a few ideas around but without much luck. They didn't have any recipe for a solution either, but we agreed on France as the only possible destination. The trouble was the French had clamped a tight lid on their borders at that moment because of the impending visit of the British royal couple. France hadn't forgotten that only four years earlier, King Alexander of Yugoslavia and French Foreign Minister Barthou had been assassinated in the streets of Marseilles during the king's visit to France.

It was dusk when I set out for home. The walk along the Limmat Quay and later on along the shore of the lake usually took about an hour. The breeze rising from the water had a soothing effect on the rumpled state of my mind. The streetlights flicked on one by one as I approached my district. The final stretch was lined with old and massive trees, effectively shielding the sidewalk from the roadway.

Which was why I hadn't noticed the black Mercedes. Suddenly it was there, sharply braking beside me as a figure jumped out. A tall, lanky man in his thirties with close-cropped hair and a protruding Adam's apple in a long neck. He moved in on me like a cat, his right hand buried in the pocket of his jacket.

"Open your mouth and I'll kill you," he said sharply, lending emphasis to his words by showing me a piece of the gun. The blue steel, dully reflecting the light of the nearest streetlamp, convinced me he meant what he said. Grabbing my arm with his free hand he pulled me toward the Mercedes.

"No tricks! The consul wants a word with you before you go back to the border. Move!"

I resisted. His face was inches from mine and the smell of beer and rotting teeth coming from his mouth nauseated me. Aiming blindly for his testicles I brought up my right knee and smashed it as hard as I could into his groin. The pain would have immobilized him long enough for me to break away—but I missed! His thigh, in a sudden shift, deflected my knee and it was more surprise than pain that made him relax his grip. He staggered back and pulled out the gun.

"Dog," he yelled, "dirty, shitty dog!"

Several years before all this occurred, in my early university days I had become interested in jujitsu. It was the fad of the moment. My instructor was a tiny Japanese, hardly five feet tall, who could break a four-inch board in two by hitting it with the edge of his palm. He took great pains to teach me how to do it too but I was never able to emulate him. I didn't even come near. But in the process I developed a pretty tough edge on my right palm. It came in handy now.

I aimed at his Adam's apple and felt the crunch as the gristle gave under the force of the blow. His mouth tore open, gaping, and an unearthly sound came from deep down in his chest as he frantically snapped for air before collapsing. The door of the Mercedes burst open. I started to run. Glancing back as I turned a corner I saw the driver kneeling beside the figure on the ground. I wondered if I had smashed his windpipe. It had felt like it. The blow had been hard enough. If so, it would mean another charge of attempted murder. The score was beginning to mount.

Still out of breath I phoned police headquarters and asked for Commissioner Schmidt. He was off duty. It took me an agonizing ten minutes to convince the placid policeman at the other end that it was a matter of life or death. He didn't believe me. He thought I was drunk. Finally I was able to wear him down and he promised to have Schmidt call me back. This he did, almost as soon as I had hung up.

He sent a police car within minutes. In the meantime we had thrown our things into the suitcases and settled up with the bewildered landlord. He didn't think I was drunk. He thought I was crazy.

Schmidt had us locked up for the night in two cells, me in one, Maria and Mother in the other. In the morning he and two plainclothesmen took us to the first train bound for Paris. We sneaked into the station through an adjoining freight shed, although the black Mercedes was nowhere in sight.

For several years after the end of the war I used to send Christmas cards to Commissioner Schmidt. I stopped the practice only after one card came back with two words scribbled across the envelope in the hand of the postman reading, "Addressee deceased."

7

Soldier of the Foreign Legion

"Gaaaaarde à vous!" yelled the corporal. The command rolled across the barracks yard like a clap of thunder. A thousand heels clicked together in a martial salute. My first Legion day had begun.

The sun of the Mediterranean looked down on Fort St. Jean in Marseilles, perched high at the top of a rock that jutted out into the sea. There was blue water as far as I could see; the low stone parapet did little to restrict the field of vision. There were sails in the breeze and gulls circled overhead.

I had arrived the night before in a convoy of several hundred volunteers. The fort, a relic from the time of the Moor invasions, was now used as a depot by the Legion, a last stop before the trip across the Mediterranean to Africa.

The night on the train had been cramped and grim. Now we were lined up, almost a thousand men, dead tired, unkempt, and dirty. There was no water to wash up. The fort was small. The sudden influx of a thousand men had knocked out the sanitary facilities—which had been rudimentary to begin with. The latrines overflowed. There was a whole ocean lapping against the foundations of the place but it hadn't occurred to the commandant that the water could be used by the men for a quick cleanup before roll call. It probably wasn't in the regulation book. So we remained unwashed—and we stank.

I hadn't slept during the endless hours on the train except for occasionally dozing off for brief periods during which my mind skipped jerkily back to the events of the preceding year. It had started with the feeling of apprehension caused by the sight of the numerous uniformed Nazi officials in the station at Basel. Commissioner Schmidt had warned me of Basel before he smuggled us onto the train. Basel was the pivot of Switzerland, Germany, and France, whose trunklines and borders converged on the town. All three countries checked passengers through the same railroad station.

Through the window I looked at the hateful uniforms and wondered if they knew about me. People had been taken off the train before by the Nazis with the Swiss unable to do anything about it, except protest to Berlin through diplomatic channels. I felt much happier when I saw a small party of French officials board the train. The leader, a young officer in smart khaki, and boots polished to a high sparkle, turned out to be a member of a special police force created to deal with the rapidly growing waves of refugees.

He saluted briskly when he entered the compartment. I handed him the passports.

"Allemand?" he asked.

Here we go again, I thought.

"Non, Monsieur, Autrichien."

He turned to his companion and engaged in a conversation in rapid French. Although I knew French from my schooldays, my ear wasn't conditioned for such speed —but I grasped the gist. To him there was no difference. The *Anschluss* was a fait accompli and he didn't see why he should let a German come into the country. The older man disagreed and pointed to the Austrian passports the young officer was still holding in his hand.

He was undecided. I had the feeling he was new on the job and needed to assert himself, or perhaps he disliked me because my blond hair and six-foot frame made me look much more the Nordic type than Hitler, Goering, Goebbels, and Himmler all rolled into one.

I began to break into a cold sweat again. I saw the Nazi garb on the far side of the tracks and I thought of the black Mercedes. I had a fleeting vision of a fat Gestapo bastard tumbling from a train in half-blind stupor. I felt a noose tightening around my neck.

But the fear was unfounded. He disliked me, there was no doubt. But he was a true Frenchman. In the heat of the discussion he hadn't paid attention to the women. Now, as he turned back to face me again, his expression clearly indicating the verdict was negative, Maria, sitting near the window, moved her head. A ray of sunshine caused her hair to erupt into a golden flame. He saw the phenomenon and his face softened. Maria's large eyes were looking straight at him. They were two luminous stars in a face tanned deeply by the sun of Zurich. Her tight blouse showed quite clearly the contours of her breasts.

Yes, he was a true Frenchman. He took in the picture. He appreciated what he saw, and a change came over him. He shook his head in wonder, as if he couldn't understand what such a beautiful woman could see in a jerk like me but then he stamped the passports, scratched his head under his kepi, saluted, and stalked out. At the door he turned and bowed in the direction of Maria.

The sun grew hotter by the minute. We had been standing at attention for an interminable length of time. The strain on the leg muscles became unbearable. Every bone in my body ached, a consequence of twenty-four sleepless hours crammed into a train as tightly as a sardine tin.

"En repos!" bellowed the corporal. He was disgusted. The officer in charge of the roll call was late. I relaxed. The feeling was heaven. We had been in Paris for a little more than a year before the war broke out. Time had moved at dizzying speed. Event after event. Each crowded out the last. Impossible to keep track. We found a small flat near the Bois de Vincennes just outside the city limits. Before we had had time to settle down and adjust, however, Hitler began to dismantle the defenses of Czechoslovakia, after having bullied Chamberlain and Daladier at Berchtesgaden into accepting his dubious promise to end all territorial claims for all time. Berchtesgaden was followed by Godesberg, Godesberg by Munich—and France mobilized.

I needed money. To earn it wasn't easy in the general turmoil. I wrote a few pieces for another news agency, drew caricatures for an anti-Nazi book published by an exiled Viennese writer, and designed sets for a small cabaret that performed in a restaurant deep in the cellars of the Louvre. It was called "Melodie Viennoise" and the pay consisted of all the goulash with dumplings and sauerkraut I could eat.

Maria joined the battle for pecuniary survival by sewing shirts for the wife of the writer whose book I illustrated. She owned a small shop. And towards the end of 1938 Maria told me she was pregnant. The event was duly celebrated with a bottle of champagne.

In March of the following year, Hitler marched into Czechoslovakia. France recalled the reservists sent home after Munich. Tanks began to rumble through the streets of Paris. In August, Hitler and Stalin signed a non-aggression pact and the Nazis invaded Poland. France proclaimed total mobilization. The street lights were painted blue to confuse enemy bombers. People were told to leave the city for the country. Paris was a boiling anthill. In the midst of the confusion François was born in a small clinic, and three days later France and Great Britain declared war on Germany. Another three days and I was en route for Marseilles, a volunteer in the French Foreign Legion for the duration of the war. Before I left I evacuated Maria and the child from the hospital while the sirens of Paris sounded the first air raid alarm.

My heart was heavy when the train pulled out. I felt guilty leaving the two women and the child, but I had no choice. The government declared anyone coming from Nazi-occupied countries an enemy alien and ordered all males interned. The only exception were army volunteers. On second thought, I realized it was the best solution to go into the army. I had wanted to fight the Nazis anyway. Now I was to be given the chance. Besides, being in the army assured the women and the child the status of a French soldier's family, which included a monthly allowance. It removed the financial problem. But it was sad I had to leave without seeing my son grow. The thought I might never see him again did not make me any happier.

The man sharing the three or four square feet of compartment floor on the way down to Marseilles wore glasses with the thickest lenses I had ever seen. He probably couldn't see at all without them. I asked him how he had managed to get into the army with such a handicap, and he chuckled.

"It was easy. Normally they wouldn't even have looked at me but now they need every man they can lay their hands on. They are so desperate they would take me as long as I can tell light from dark."

He was German. His name was Fritz von Falkenau he spoke flawless French. He had the face of an intellectual, emphasized by the heavy, hornrimmed glasses straddling the bridge of a sharp, slightly oversized nose

63

under a perpetual frown. When he stood up I saw he was short, but the uniform they had given him was several sizes too big. I couldn't remember ever having seen a less soldierly looking soldier. Another edition of *The Brave Soldier Schwejk,* I thought.

Shortly after my talk with von Falkenau I dozed off again. His name played games with my subconscious. Somehow it had struck a chord in my memory. What it was eluded me for a while but then I remembered. There had been another von Falkenau, a prominent German politician who was assassinated in the early twenties by two terrorists. The killers managed to get away, but the body of one of them was found the following day near the tracks of the trunkline leading into France. He had been shot through the head. The bullets matched those found in von Falkenau's body.

The other killer, considered more dangerous, had disappeared, leaving no trace. For a while police were looking for him all over Europe but he was never found. It was assumed he had killed his accomplice for fear of betrayal. The newspapers were full of the story for weeks. Finally it had petered out.

Coincidence, I thought. A similarity of names. There must be thousands of von Falkenaus in Germany. It wasn't an uncommon name.

And now, some twenty-four hours later I was standing under the sky of the Midi with the hot sun beating down on my heavy tunic, an unwashed Legionnaire with red-rimmed eyes and a three-day-old beard, waiting for an officer to put an end to the agony of my first military roll call. Beside me in the line of tired men stood von Falkenau. For some reason he had attached himself to me and followed me like a dog seeking assurance from his master. He looked like a wise old owl under the weight of the heavy glasses dominating his features.

The officer finally came. He was an adjutant-chief, the

highest noncommissioned officer in the French army and the highest rank a foreigner can attain in the Legion—with a few specific exceptions. He was tall and well built, with broad shoulders although he was slightly stooped, probably from too many years of hostile climate, too much booze on top of malaria and yellow fever, too many white nights with the whores of Africa and Indo-China. Perhaps dope too. Or venereal disease. His posture was that of a bored man, but his eyes contradicted the impression. Light, almost colorless, they seemed incapable of emotion. I thought of the eyes of a cobra: cold, impersonal—and deadly.

Out front, a cluster had formed around the tall adjutant-chief. The corporal yelled another sharp "Garde à vous!" and again we snapped to rigid attention. He began to rattle off names and every time a name was called its bearer yelled "Présent!" It went much smoother than I had thought. There were at least twenty, perhaps even thirty languages in the contingent but it didn't slow down the performance. Those unable to speak French already knew the way the noncoms fractured their alien names and yelled "Présent!" every time they heard the sound. There wasn't a single hitch until the corporal came to Fritz von Falkenau.

Fritz yelled his "Présent!" The corporal ticked off his name on the list and was already calling the next when the tall adjutant-chief motioned him to stop. He took the list from the corporal's hand, studied it for a moment, and gave it back. The corporal took this for a signal to continue, but the adjutant-chief stopped him.

"Wait," he said. He said something else, which I couldn't hear because of the distance. The corporal bellowed von Falkenau's name again and Fritz echoed back with another "Présent!" I thought there had been a momentary hesitation in his voice before he answered but I could have been mistaken.

The adjutant-chief, having pinpointed Fritz's position,

set out in his direction, pushing briskly through the dense throngs of men. We watched his progress in complete silence. The harbor rumbled in the background. The officer shoved the last two men separating him from his target aside and planted himself in front of Fritz. Tall, vigorous, feet apart, he towered over the unhappy figure of the recruit. He stared down at Fritz for several interminable minutes. Still at attention, I turned my head slightly to get the full picture.

"What's your name again?" asked the officer.

"Légionnaire, deuxième classe, Falkenau, mon Adjutant-chef. Fritz von Falkenau."

"Von Falkenau," said the officer flatly, nodding several times as if the repetition of the name had confirmed a lingering doubt.

Fritz stood stiffly, his body rigid under the sagging, oversized tunic and the ridiculous baggy pants. But I could feel the tension in him. He was stretched taut like a bow just before the release of the arrow. He reminded me of a cornered animal poised to go for the enemy's jugular.

The adjutant-chief did not seem to notice the effect he had had on Fritz. "Do you know me?" he asked.

"Oui, mon Adjutant-chef," said Fritz.

A grin spread slowly across the handsome face of the tall man. It was not a pleasant grin. It was a sneer, a sadistic twist of his cheek muscles, deepened by two prominent grooves that furrowed from his nostrils to the edges of the mouth. The adjutant-chief was visibly amused. Fritz's face, as much as I could see from the corner of my eye, was impassive.

"You do? Well, tell me. Who am I?"

Fritz remained silent. Stiff and rigid, he did not move. He seemed petrified, staring into the cold snake eyes of the man before him.

The officer grew impatient. The grin disappeared. The contours of his cheeks hardened and the chin jutted out.

"Speak up!" he said sharply. "Say it! This is an order! Who am I?"

For a moment Fritz did not move. But then, very subtly, his posture changed. He relaxed, as if a heavy burden had miraculously been removed from his shoulders. When he answered, his voice was calm and even, but this time there was a sharp edge of hatred in it. Not the boiling, red-hot hatred that prompts one to do foolish things on the spur of the moment, but the cold and deliberate hatred which, nursed over many years, turns into a deep and dominating obsession.

"You are my father's murderer, mon Adjutant-chef," said Fritz evenly.

His voice was loud and clear and it carried from one end of the yard to the other. A sharp rustle of surprise broke the tension and swept through the lines. For several seconds, the adjutant-chief did not move. He continued to stare into Fritz's eyes and Fritz returned the stare calmly. The sneer was back on the tall man's face. Suddenly, without warning he pivoted on his heels and clapped his hands in a signal to the corporal to continue the roll call.

I don't know what ever became of Fritz von Falkenau. We were separated in Sidi-bel-Abbès and assigned to different units. The war continued and I don't know where they sent him. But it was about two years later that I ran into a Legionnaire who had been in my contingent at the time of the incident at Fort St. Jean. He had just returned from Meknès, the Moroccan garrison town reputed for its red light district, said to be the largest in the world. He told me that the tall adjutant-chief had been found dead in a whore's room with a bullet in his head. The official story had been suicide, but it was rumored that the bullet had entered the head from the neck and no one had ever seen a suicide who would shoot himself through the neck. Besides, they didn't find the gun.

He also mentioned that Fritz von Falkenau's unit had passed through Meknès on its way south at about the time of the adjutant-chief's suicide. In fact, von Falkenau's contingent had stayed on in town for three days before moving on.

Of course it could have been coincidence, the kind of coincidence that traditionally puzzles the sleuth in a mystery story. But then again it was quite possible that von Falkenau, placed in the same locale at the same time as his father's killer, saw the one and only chance of a lifetime to even the score with the man he so fiercely hated. I am inclined to think von Falkenau did the killing, because at that time I had already realized that nothing was impossible in the Legion. Life in the Legion was unbelievable, incongruous, lacking plausibility. Each day brought another surprise and more often than not the surprise was death when least expected. Tension was never absent. It was comparable to stepping gingerly through a minefield. One careless move and you were blown sky-high.

The all-pervading tension, however, had one beneficial advantage: it forced me to take my mind off my preoccupation with the fate of Maria, François, Mother, and my brother. Besides, the Legion is a self-contained unit. You are shut off from the outside world, especially in the remote outposts which dot the sands of the desert. You live in a cocoon, concerned only with day-to-day survival. Everything else becomes unimportant. Suddenly the war in Europe became strangely unreal, as if it had nothing whatsoever to do with me. Everything was so far away—the Nazis, the women, my son. They faded into the background, dislodged from my mind by the immediacy of self-preservation and my determination to stay alive. An old Legion general once coined the phrase that death always marches with the Legion and as corny as it sounds he had a good point.

I don't know whether Jerome would have agreed with

the general if he had lived, but just as I will never know whether the adjutant-chief blew out his own brains in an alcoholic stupor or Fritz von Falkenau did it for him, I will never know what killed Jerome.

When the mule kicked Jerome, the temperature was already 110 and it was still early in the day.

It happened in the middle of nowhere. The air was so hot the sand flickered before my eyes. The mule had been suffering from the heat too or it wouldn't have kicked Jerome, who was always gentle with animals. The sharp hoof hit him just above the stomach and drove the wind from his lungs. For a moment, wide-eyed surprise showed in Jerome's face as if he couldn't believe what was happening to him. Then he gasped "Nom de Dieu!" and collapsed with a groan. I tried to help him up and he strained to struggle to his feet, but he couldn't. He fell back thrashing in the sand, his arms clutching his stomach.

Lieutenant Crozier was standing a few feet away talking to Sergeant Tetrazeh. His back was turned and he hadn't seen anything. Then he noticed the commotion and walked over to Jerome.

"What happened?" he asked. I told him.

"Where did he get it? In the balls?"

I thought it had been too high for that and said so. Crozier bent down. He opened Jerome's tunic and pulled up the shirt. There was nothing to see except for a reddish spot where the hoof had connected. The lieutenant ran his fingers along the ribcage and found the ribs intact. Then he pressed his thumb into the red spot and Jerome howled with pain. Crozier remained unimpressed.

"Help him up," he said. "Nothing broken. He'll be all right."

Crozier was a fine young officer, a product of France's best military schools. Unfortunately, his medical knowledge was nonexistent. He saw neither a bleeding wound nor a broken bone. All he saw was a reddish spot which happened to be sensitive to the touch. He had no doubt the man would be all right even if he was in pain. Legionnaires were trained to stand pain. After a while the pain would go away. It was also obvious Lieutenant Crozier had never been kicked in the guts by a mule.

Helped by another man, I grabbed Jerome under his arm pits and together we managed to hoist him up. He was heavy and tried to cooperate, but once on his feet, an apologetic look came into his eyes. His knees buckled, his body became limp, and he dropped back into the sand. This time he was out cold.

I looked at Crozier. "No use, mon Lieutenant," I said unnecessarily. "He's conked out."

On a forced march under battle conditions, a Legion unit is not allowed to alter marching orders. We were on just such a forced march. Nothing was permitted to slow us down. In cases like this an incapacitated Legionnaire is left behind with food and water to last him a few days and is expected to follow his unit as soon as his handicap permits it. Such is the law of the Legion. But Jerome was a valuable man. He was the only mule specialist in the outfit and Crozier knew it was imperative to have him restored to effectiveness without delay. He decided to compromise.

A circle had formed. The lieutenant looked at me. "Martin," he said, "he's your pal, isn't he?"

"Yes, mon Lieutenant."

"Bien," said Crozier. "You stay with him. Join us as soon as he can walk." He pivoted on his heels and looked at the faces around him. What he saw was a group of grimy, sweating soldiers. He pointed at the man nearest him.

"You too, he said. "Give Martin a hand."

With the jangle and clatter of rifles and equipment hoisted to shoulders, the detachment moved on. I watched the slowly meandering file until it reached the horizon. The men grew smaller and smaller, sometimes hidden by the swell of the dunes, then coming into view again. One by one, they finally disappeared behind the last rise.

Jerome was by this time very pale. There was a trace of bloody foam at the corners of his mouth but his breathing seemed normal. The kick had probably ripped something inside and he was hemorrhaging. But there didn't seem to be any fever and I thought I would wait until nightfall and move on after the heat of the day was gone. By then I hoped Jerome would have recouped some of his strength.

There was one problem however: we were in hostile Arab country. There had not been any trouble for years but Nazi agents had been able to infiltrate some of the nomadic tribes in the more remote regions of Algeria and Morocco. Ambushes, sporadic raids, and sabotage were on the increase. And we were miles away from the nearest military post. There was always the chance of roving horsemen showing up. They would be delighted to find three isolated Legionnaires who some time later would be discovered by a search party disembowelled and their balls cut off as had happened countless times in the past. It wasn't exactly a pleasant prospect.

We took turns. I stayed with Jerome while the other Legionnaire kept watch and from time to time we changed places. Nothing happened all day. Jerome dozed and there was no sign of Arabs, hostile or friendly. That was not really surprising. If there were Arabs in the area they wouldn't attempt anything—in broad daylight anyway. I hadn't noticed anything unusual or suspicious and I thought that was a good sign. With a sick man on my hands I could do without additional trouble.

The Arabs fooled me. They had probably been there all the time, hidden or camouflaged or too far away for me to detect them. Just as I thought, they waited for nightfall. Darkness comes fast in the desert. It was my time for the watch. Just as the sun dipped below the rim of the desert, my ears caught a sound that did not belong to the scene and in a reflex movement I dove behind a rock. Not a second too soon. Dust and splinters covered me before I heard the shots. I had seen the flashes of their rifles and let loose with my sub. There was a shrill outcry, followed by more shots.

My companion joined the act and emptied his automatic in the direction of the attackers. There were more yells of pain and then a clatter of hooves which quickly faded into the distance. They left two dead behind, whom we found later.

But Jerome was dead too. A bullet had ripped through his throat. It was a fatal wound and yet I've never known what really killed him, the mule or the bullet. For all I know he could have been dead from internal bleeding before the Arabs attacked. I know it was a moot point and didn't bother Jerome anymore but it puzzled me all the same. The general was probably right when he said in the Legion you walk with death. The fear is always with you. You look over your shoulder at every step until you reach a point where you surrender to the fatalism of the Muslim and his philosophy of *Kismet* which is anchored in his religion. *Kismet* means fate, and the Koran says *mektoub,* "it is written," and there is no escape. Which was obviously very true in the case of Jerome, but infinitely more so for Simon Borgmeester, the Dutchman.

Simon had been in my company only for a short spell but even in the limited time he was with us he managed to drive everybody crazy. There was no doubt he was a neurotic—a condition the Legion language translates into the word *cafard,* meaning "bug." A man afflicted with *cafard* has bugs in his brain. *Cafard* manifests itself in many forms. In Simon it was triggered by a Gypsy woman, who, after reading his palm, told him he wouldn't get out of the Legion alive. This so frightened

72

the shit out of Simon that he nearly strangled the woman and had to be dragged away from her screaming and kicking and foaming at the mouth. The woman took it calmly. It wasn't her fault he was going to die, she said. She told him only what she had seen in his palm. It was all there. She hadn't made it up. *Mektoub!*

It is possible that Simon had been a borderline mental case all along and probably deeply superstitious into the bargain. The Gypsy had unbalanced him just a little more and when he calmed down he swore he would show that "filthy whore of a Gypsy" a thing or two. He was going to get out of the Legion alive, come hell or high water. But the prediction preyed on his mind. He talked about it incessantly and finally everybody began to avoid him. After a while the men who shared sleeping quarters with him told him to shut up or they would make sure the Gypsy's prediction came true. After that he kept silent, which was a blessing. His high-pitched, whining voice had made the evenings unbearable.

Simon was in a good position to cheat the Gypsy. His five years in the Legion were almost up. He had just a few more weeks remaining when the woman read his palm and because of her curse he refused to renew his contract for another stretch.

Simon's story would hardly have been worth telling if it hadn't been for the way he died. If John O'Hara had heard about it, it might have inspired him to write a sequel to *Appointment in Samarra.* There was a young Spaniard in the company, a reject from the Spanish Civil War. His name was José Francisco Alvarez but we called him Franco for short. Franco was gun-crazy. He had been in Tunisia during the mass surrender of the Italian army and somehow had gotten hold of one of the latest Italian 9 mm submachine guns, which looked like the mating of an American short carbine, a British Sten gun, and a German Schmeisser. It was something he had always wanted. Ignoring orders to the contrary, he disassembled it and hid the parts in his pack.

On one of the hottest days of the year and after the colonel had reinstated the noon siesta abolished at the outbreak of the war, twenty men were stretched out on their cots in the barracks. The shades were drawn tight except for a small crack to permit enough light for Franco who was just assembling his prize possession, the Italian sub. Lying on the cot next to his, I watched his nimble fingers. Every piece found its logical place in the assembly, just as in a jigsaw puzzle. Franco knew what he was doing. Finally, the last part in the place where it belonged, Franco lifted the barrel to his shoulder and peered through the sight.

"Ah," he said, "what balance, what beauty."

He sat down on my cot.

"See," he said. "Two triggers. I have it all figured out. The front trigger is for continuous shooting, the other for single shots. It's just the opposite from ours and the English subs. It will take a while to get used to it."

He slammed a clip into the breech.

"You are not going to load it," I said.

"Just to get the feel," he said. "Just to see how she balances."

"Don't touch the trigger," I said.

"Don't fret. The catch is on. See!"

But the catch wasn't on. It too worked in an unfamiliar way. When Franco touched the trigger, the gun burped. The bullets hit the wall and twenty men jumped from their beds in panic. Franco had pulled the trigger he thought released only one shot at a time. It turned out it was the one that controlled continuous action. Besides, it was a hair trigger. The slightest touch emptied the whole magazine.

Corporal Castagnet stormed into the room, livid.

"You stupid bastard!" he bellowed. He reached for the

gun but Franco wouldn't let go. Castagnet used his second hand to wrench the weapon from Franco and in the process touched the trigger designed to release one bullet only. It too was a hair trigger. The gun burped again, but just once this time.

In spite of the commotion I heard a fierce outcry outside and rushed to the window pulling up the shade. There was a neat hole in the glass with cracks radiating from it in symmetrical order. On the flagstones below the window lay a still figure in civilian clothes. Simon Borgmeester lay dead. The bullet had gone into his left temple and out the other side. Both holes were small and round and clean and bled very little. It was a powerful gun.

Simon Borgmeester was buried in his civilian suit. In his breast pocket he had his discharge papers and in his wallet there was the faded picture of a full-breasted blonde woman holding an infant in her arms. There was also a thousand francs in new bills, the final bonus a Legionnaire collects on the day of his discharge.

8

Assault on Narvik

When the ammunition truck blew up it left a jagged crater in the road and flattened every building nearby.

It was never established how many people died in the collapsed houses. An undetermined number of Arab children, attracted to the truck by curiosity typical of children everywhere, disappeared in the conflagration, as did the six Legionnaires aboard the truck. Nor was it ever known what had caused the explosion. It could have been a careless Legionnaire smoking a cigarette in violation of regulations and common sense, or a sniper pumping a bullet into the ammunition, or simply unstable nitro.

The explosion had occurred on a hot morning halfway between Oran and Sidi-bel-Abbès, on a secondary road that winds through a number of villages populated by Arabs and colons of Spanish descent. The truck was the last in a convoy of six traveling in intervals of several hundred feet. Luckily the drivers had maintained the prescribed distance or the whole convoy would have blown up in a domino effect.

Lieutenant Flavelle ordered the convoy stopped at a safe distance from the blast and raced back to the scene. The devastation was complete. Shouts and screams for help were coming from some of the damaged houses but Flavelle was interested only in the military side. The civilian aspect was not his concern.

I owed my own life to an act of insubordination. Although under strict orders not to leave the ammunition truck under any circumstances, we had stopped in front of a mud hut, where a sign in French and Arabic said beer was sold. I had rushed in to fetch a few bottles and was just rushing out again when the truck blew up.

Flavelle ordered a quick search of the houses in an effort to determine the fate of the crew, which was my lucky break because the search party found me buried under three feet of debris. Everybody was surprised to find me alive—including myself. It was a miracle. I had only a few bruises, some bleeding scratches, and an egg-shaped lump on the forehead. I was still stunned when they pulled me from the pile of masonry and broken stones and when I tried to get on my feet, my right knee refused to function. Flavelle assumed it was busted and ordered me evacuated to the military hospital at Saida.

At the hospital the bed next to mine was occupied by a Legionnaire named Kasimir Kolaczkowski. He had been stung by a poisonous insect which caused his left foot to swell up to three times its normal size. As no one was able to pronounce Kasimir's name comfortably he was generally known as K.K.

K.K. was about my age and like me he had enlisted at the outbreak of the war. He spoke French fluently with the musical accent peculiar to many Slavs and while he didn't talk much about his background he mentioned once that he had been a captain in the Polish army before being forced to flee from Poland and that he was now waiting for a similar commission in the Legion. The French government, he said, was going to give foreign volunteers the same rank they held in their native armies. I thought that was merely a case of wishful thinking on the part of K.K. but it turned out I was mistaken.

My knee wasn't broken after all, just a torn ligament and some peripheral damage. Captain Durand, the hospital's chief medic, said it would heal spontaneously given enough rest. He didn't even have to cut. He put the leg in a cast and I was given a pair of crutches. K.K. was walking with crutches too, which created a sympathetic bond between us, but I only began to know him better the night they brought in two black Senegalese soldiers left behind by their regiment en route to the European front. Both had pneumonia and were delirious when they were wheeled into our room.

Marguerite Hauteserre, the head nurse, who ruled the ward with a fist of iron, blew into the room like a sandstorm.

"K.K.," she said to Kasimir, "you take care of this one," pointing to the older of the two negroes who was in a coma.

"I can hardly move," Kasimir protested.

"Je m'en fiche," said Marguerite, unimpressed. "That's an order!" She had the rank of lieutenant.

"You," she added, turning to me. "You look after the other!" and without another word she sailed out of the room, her full skirt billowing in her wake.

My patient was a young, ebony-black giant nearly seven feet tall and very sick. His name was Djiri Coulibali. For two days and two nights I waited on him hand and foot, wiping his burning forehead, changing his bedclothes, feeding him, emptying his bedpan, and doing the thousand things one does for a delirious person. After two days his temperature dropped dramatically, which made me the happiest man in the hospital because I was completely exhausted. Penicillin would have cured his fever in a matter of hours but that drug wasn't invented until about two years later.

Kasimir worked just as hard but his man died in the third night. Coulibali snapped out of his delirium and bounced back as if he had never been sick.

A few days later we were sitting in the hospital garden, Kasimir, Djiri Coulibali and I and Djiri said he was the son of a powerful tribal chief and had six wives back home. He also said he was grateful to me. Somehow he remembered, despite the delirium.

"You very good to Djiri Coulibali," he said. "You first white man good to me."

"Skip it," I said. "You would have done the same."

"Maybe," he said. "But Djiri Coulibali very grateful. Djiri Coulibali show you how grateful. I give you wife. She youngest wife. She big and strong and good worker. She make good children."

"Splendid," I said. I did not tell him I already had a wife. It wouldn't have made any difference to him anyway. This was his way of thanking me. His simple nature wouldn't have understood a refusal. We agreed I would pick up the wife after the war and he gave me detailed instructions on how to find his village. It was all very simple.

Djiri Coulibali was discharged from the hospital the following morning. I watched him as he walked out the gate, tall, narrow-hipped, with powerful shoulders, and very bewildered. K.K.'s foot had returned to normal. The night before he left we smuggled a few bottles of wine into the hospital and got roaring drunk. The next morning he joined his company. I watched him go, his musette slung over his shoulder and limping slightly.

My turn came a week later. By now the war was almost nine months old and I hadn't seen the enemy once. At least not the Nazis. I had been in several scraps in North Africa but it had all been of a minor nature—police action more than anything else. Pacifying rebellious tribes and dealing with small ambush activity and local snipers. And then there had been that thing with Jerome.

The day came sooner than I expected. I had hardly arrived back at my company when it became obvious something out of the ordinary was happening. Confirmation came through almost immediately. We had been assigned to the 13th Demi-Brigade of the First Regiment of the Legion. Demi-Brigade was a euphemism for march battalion. It meant we were slated for the front.

I was puzzled however when I turned in my uniform for a new outfit. I assumed we were going to France where it was now spring, but the new uniform was heavy and warm, with a fur-lined olive-green parka as the pièce de résistance, complimented by gloves and woolen underwear. I asked the sergeant who was supervising the transaction why we were getting winter uniforms when it was going to be summer in another few weeks. He shrugged and gave me the standard Legion reply: "Ne cherchez pas à comprendre!" Don't try to understand.

The mystery deepened after our troopship left Oran and instead of heading for Marseilles, turned west and passed Gibraltar for the open Atlantic. It was only after the BBC shortwave radio began talking about a Nazi invasion of Norway that the picture became less muddled. It seemed the 13th Demi-Brigade had been elected to kick the Nazis out of Norway, which they had occupied in April 1940 to secure the iron ore of Narvik, desperately needed to keep the Nazi war machine going.

That was the reason I was now aboard a ship that had seen better days, crammed with more than two-thousand men hastily recruited from several Legion regiments, and equipped with weapons most of us were not familiar with. I was given a new type of submachine gun, a mixture of Czech design and British manufacture which I had never seen before, but a crash course on the high seas taught me how to use it. I liked it. It was light and accurate and deadly. It fired a whole clip in a matter of seconds. I also got a new kind of egg-shaped hand grenade with frightening explosive force. The grenade was frightening in another respect as well. You had only seven seconds after you activated the thing. If you still had it in your hand it would blow you to smithereens.

There was a new man in my section, who had arrived while I was at the hospital. He said his name was Pierre Lamontagne, which was hard to believe. He said he had come to Paris from a ghetto in Galicia in the early thirties and had probably changed his name for reasons of expediency. Lamontagne had been in the Legion before, having served five years plus an additional year in the penal battalion for stealing Legion uniforms and selling them to Arab merchants. He hated the Legion but because he had been discharged as a reservist at the end of his contract, he had now been recalled. Besides his hatred of the Legion the only thought that occupied his mind was how to get out of the Corps.

Corporal Castagnet had it in for Pierre Lamontagne. He had known him from his first stretch and there was no love lost between the two. Castagnet never wasted a chance to rile Pierre. The new submachine gun was a godsend for Castagnet. He made Pierre take it apart, clean it, oil it, and reassemble it so many times the men in the section watching the game lost track of the number. Finally, Pierre had had enough.

"Clean it yourself, Castagnet," he said.

"Are you refusing to obey an order?" asked Castagnet, who had prayed for just such an opportunity.

"Stick it up your ass," said Pierre.

"You will be reported."

"Je t'emmerde," said Pierre. "I shit on you."

Castagnet reported Pierre, who was stuck in the hole for forty-eight hours on bread and water and no cigarettes—which did not exactly enhance Pierre's fighting spirit. When he came out of the hole his eyes were bloodshot and he was in a murderous mood. His bunk was on top of mine and I could hear him mumble obscenities with Castagnet as the center piece. I think he thought of faking an accident at the next shooting exercise and emptying his clip into Castagnet instead of the target.

But the intended homicide never materialized: Pierre was sidetracked. The morning after his release, a small gunboat caught up with us and delivered several bags of mail, which was a pleasant surprise. There had not been any mail since we left Africa. It was no pleasant surprise for Pierre, however: he had received only one piece of mail, a laconic note from the Red Cross in Geneva which his wife had forwarded from Oran. In crisp terms the note notified him that his entire family back in Poland had been exterminated together with the rest of the village's population.

Pierre was sitting on a coil of rope reading the letter. His face was chalk white and he was crying.

The colonel was strutting up and down the deck with Captain Charpentier when he noticed Pierre.

"Some Legionnaire," he said with disgust. "He is crying. Some soldier."

"Debout!" barked Charpentier. "Get up!"

Pierre rose slowly. The note dangled from his limp hand. The colonel reached for it and read it. Death had never fazed the colonel, but this time he deviated. Perhaps he was getting old and soft. He put his hand on Pierre's shoulder and looked at him for a few silent seconds.

"Tough luck, soldier," he said finally, "C'est la guerre," and he resumed his walk.

The ship had moved steadily north. A strange change had come over the sky, which for several days had refused to turn completely dark at night. In fact the nights became faintly lighter until there was no darkness at all but just a milky haziness without shadows and contrasts. We had entered the region of the midnight sun.

So far no one had had a precise idea of where we were going. We could only guess. Then Lieutenant Richard assembled the section for a briefing. We were headed for Norway, he said, and in particular for Narvik in the north, because the Nazis had jumped the gun on the Allies and occupied the port. It so happened that Narvik was of the greatest strategic importance. The possession of the port could influence the outcome of the whole war. It was the only port through which the Nazis could ship Swedish iron ore and steel essential for their war effort. If Narvik was taken the flow of steel would dry up. No more tanks for Germany, no more trucks, no more artillery. It was imperative that the port be returned to us.

Richard explained that the British Navy was keeping close watch on the shipping lanes up and down the rugged Norwegian coast and had intercepted and sunk several ore carriers on their way to Germany. More vessels had slipped through the net, however, than the British were able to catch. The only way to stop the Nazis was to take Narvik.

All that sounded reasonable enough. But it wasn't going to be easy. The entrance to Narvik was protected by a formation of mountains, spiked with Nazi artillery batteries. A frontal assault on the port was out of the question. The only way to assault Narvik was by land and it had therefore been decided to land troops north and south of the town and perform a pincer movement that would trap the German garrison in the port. We, the 13th Demi-Brigade, were to attack from the south while the rest of the expeditionary force was to attack from the north. Once the two beachheads were established, both pincer arms were to push on to Narvik and join forces. It sounded simple enough.

The place selected for the attack was a fjord, whose geological formation seemed favorable for a landing, just a few miles south of Narvik. Reconnaissance planes had reported the existence of only one Nazi battery in the mountain that overshadowed the fjord but it was not seen as an obstacle. The landing force was to be protected by a British battleship, which would not only screen the fleet of landing boats from the Nazi gunners but was also supposed to put the enemy battery out of action with its own heavy guns.

That sounded simple too. That it didn't turn out that way may not have been due to faulty planning; it may have been a combination of exaggerated optimism and bad luck, but whatever it was, the strategy was to cause the premature deaths of two-thousand men.

Less than forty-eight hours later a British battleship leading the parade steamed into the narrow fjord, followed by our transport and a few auxiliary vessels. The scene was painted in an eery, opaque whiteness. A thin milky mist floated on the water, the black outlines of the craggy mountains pressing in from all sides barely visible. The battleship moved cautiously in the direction of the farthest shore of the fjord. We followed closely behind. When the big ship came to a stop, we began to lower the boats.

The water was deep and black and it was several

hundred feet to the shore. There was no beach except for a few narrow strips of rock flattened by the action of the waves. The boats had to go straight into shore. It took about half an hour for the men to fill the boats. Everything went smoothly at first. A serene stillness lay over the fjord, interrupted only by the cries of the gulls circling angrily overhead. The order to push off came and the boats' engines began to roar. There were about twenty or twenty-five sturdy lifeboats, each loaded to the hilt with men and material. Some were sitting so deep the waterline was just a few inches below the boats' rim, but the sea was calm. There was no danger of being swamped.

My boat had already covered half the distance between ship and shore when I heard a dull bang somewhere above us in the mountains, and almost simultaneously the sound of an explosion aboard the battleship.

"Merde," mumbled Lieutenant Richard who was just a few feet away from me in the compact mass of soldiers filling the boat. "The Boches. They're shooting, the bastards!"

He yelled to the helmsman to open the throttle and the boat jerked forward in a sudden spray. I saw commotion aboard the battleship. The big guns in the turrets turned smoothly in the direction the German battery was assumed to be entrenched but before they could go into action the Nazis scored another hit. There was a blinding flash as the conning tower was hit. The subsequent explosion of ammunition wrapped everything in a cloud of black and yellow smoke. The big ship trembled from bow to stern as it backed up under full engine pressure to get out of reach of the guns. Flames were shooting from the tower.

The Nazi gunners, apparently realizing the battleship had ceased to be a threat for the moment, now concentrated on the boats. Geysers sprouted left and right. There was no need for direct hits. A near hit was sufficient. The waves caused by the impact swamped the heavily loaded boats, spilling the men into the water. The near-freezing temperature of the air and water did the rest: in their heavy winter gear, loaded down with equipment, the men did not have a chance. The cold paralyzed them in a matter of seconds. Rescue was impossible. Heads bobbed up and down in the water, faces distorted in agonizing shouts for help as we passed them.

There were a few direct hits. Slicks of blood spread from the splintered boats and more capsized. One by one the bobbing heads disappeared below the surface while my boat sped toward the shore. As far as I could see, there was only one other boat still intact which was now racing at top speed toward the opposite shore of the fjord. It was loaded with about sixty men and several machine guns. They were headed for an overhang which would have provided shelter from the guns. They never made it. The boat was hit and disintegrated in an explosion of flying wood and bodies. Several heads were seen swimming toward the shore but they too disappeared gradually.

The boats had been slated to return to the mother ship for the rest of the 13th Demi-Brigade but they were all gone with the exception of one. The plan had gone sour and it was now up to the colonel to find ways and means to land the other half of the contingent. But the Nazis took the problem out of the colonel's hands. They fired a round into the transport with deadly precision. Some shells hit the superstructure with devastating effect and then they managed a few good hits below the water line. We had just reached shore and were crawling out of the boat and under the rocks, when the troop ship began to list. In the absence of boats, the men jumped into the water hoping to be rescued by the battleship, but the hope was a futile one. The big ship, preoccupied with its own fate, was steaming at full speed toward the mouth of the fjord, yellow flames shooting from the conning tower.

It had taken only a few minutes but the assault forces of the 13th Demi-Brigade had ceased to exist—with the exception of three or four dozen men who now huddled on a narrow strip of land between the edge of the water and a steep mountain.

Lieutenant Richard took stock. He had forty-three men left, including himself. If he was shaken by what had just happened, he did not show it. He had been a Legion officer all his adult life and he knew his duty. His orders were to attack the invading forces from the south and that was what he was going to do, even if he had to do it alone. Single-handedly if necessary, although it was suicide. But such was the code of the Legion and Richard was a courageous man.

He was also a madman. He was bound by a rigid timetable. The various phases of the attack had been worked out in detail. At precisely 1600 hours an RAF squadron was scheduled to bombard the approaches to Narvik to soften up the Nazi defenses. Richard did not know if the plan was still on the books, considering the disastrous result of the landing, and tried to get through to the colonel. But the small portable radio transmitter produced only crackling static in the operator's headphones. So, in the absence of orders to the contrary, Richard considered it his holy duty to continue the war.

There was only one noncom in the group, a Sergeant Mueller, a powerfully built man of forty whose ribbons indicated a long and colorful career. Richard and Mueller went into a prolonged huddle.

We were sitting at the bottom of a gully cut into the rock by the water coming down from the mountain. At the moment there were only ice and snow patches mixed in with rocks and debris in the ditch, no water. As far as I could determine, the Nazi battery was perched some 1,500 feet in the center of the U-shaped mountain formation that encased three sides of the fjord. The gully, rising to the same height and beyond, veered slightly away from the battery emplacement. It was the only way to the guns and if Richard wanted to take them, the assault had to come through the gully.

Lieutenant Richard may have been a madman but he knew his business. His orders were quick and precise. Mueller was to take half the contingent, transfer to the opposite side of the fjord, and move up the mountain with the purpose of detracting the gunners' attention, while Richard, with the rest of us, was to use the protection of the gully to approach from the other side. It was an insane plan. We had no idea of the Nazis' strength. They could have had a whole regiment up there. Nor did we know how they were armed. A single machine gun could abort the whole thing.

I watched Mueller and his men cautiously crawl across the open stretch that separated us from the far side of the fjord. As soon as they started to climb, we moved into the gully. We too began to climb. The Nazis couldn't see us. We were protected by the unevenness of the ground and the depressions washed out by the water at the bottom of the gully. But they could see Mueller's men and fired at them sporadically. I heard only single shots sounding like carbines. Good, I thought, no machine gun.

We moved up quickly. The realization that they didn't have a machine gun elated me. It made things much easier. Perhaps Richard's plan wasn't so insane after all. Perhaps there was only a handful to cope with and we would be able to eliminate them quickly. After all, we were all trained in hand-to-hand combat. I felt a fleeting affection for Sergeant Tetrazeh who had taught me how to gore a man with my bayonet. Not even the sudden realization that my sub wasn't built for a bayonet could dim my gratitude to him.

My optimism was premature: they did have a machine gun. One of the latest models that fired a thousand rounds a minute. They had been waiting for the right moment, which came when Mueller's men had to traverse a flat stretch that resembled a landing in a flight of giant steps. There was no protection; they would be out in the open.

Mueller knew it was a dangerous spot but he too seemed to have been thinking in terms of rifle fire to oppose him and in the tradition of desert combat he ordered his men to fan out and cross the danger point at high speed. His thinking would have been correct in the desert, facing poorly armed, emotional Arab tribesmen shooting from horseback. He didn't know he was being watched by a highly trained marksman behind the visor of one of the deadliest machine guns of the period. The gunner had anticipated Mueller's intention and waited patiently for the sergeant's two dozen men to emerge onto the plateau.

As soon as they were out in the open he let go and the men went down like domino pieces. One of the first was Mueller. Two or three others managed to jump into holes or hide behind rocks while others crawled painfully toward shelter. A few made it; some were hit again and died where they lay.

Richard kept silent. Only his lips contracted to one thin, straight line and the skin around his cheekbones had gone white. But he couldn't keep still.

"Sales cochons," I heard him mumble. "Dirty swine." He continued to mumble while he gestured to us to continue the climb.

After another fifteen or twenty minutes of painful wriggling on my belly or crouching on all fours along the bottom of the ditch where the Nazis couldn't see me, I finally saw the machine gun. It was sitting in front of four cannons mounted on halftracks and placed in a half circle. The platform was man-made and formed an apron around the mouth of a tunnel leading into the interior of the mountain. Ten or twelve soldiers were busying themselves with the artillery pieces. The machine gunner sat stolidly behind his contraption. They had no idea we were there. Mueller's detraction scheme was paying off. But there was also the chance they pretended not to see us to lure us into a more vulnerable position. This was a mistake because we now had them within range of our own weapons.

"Shoot!" Richard said simply and we opened up.

The machine gunner went down immediately. He had been sitting there immobile, an ideal target. The rest of them hit the ground and Richard thought the time had come to take the battery in one daring assault across the rock-littered slope. Before we could get into action, however, the machine gun was chattering again. The gunner had been replaced. We jumped back behind the rocks that formed the sides of the ditch. The delay was bad. It gave them a breathing spell which they used with great efficiency.

They must have had some other weapon up there on the platform, a mortar-like thing able to lob grenades with relative accuracy. Whatever it was it nearly finished the southern pincer of the assault force on Narvik. It also set a temporary end to Lieutenant Richard's career. I heard a plop just behind us followed by an earth-shattering explosion. Debris flew in all directions. When the smoke cleared half of the men were on the ground, some dead, some bleeding. As far as I could tell I wasn't hurt but I was sure my eardrums had burst. Richard had been hurled several feet and was bleeding from a wound in his forehead. His right eye was a pulpy mess and both of his legs were twisted at a crazy angle, but he was alive and conscious. I crawled to his side.

"Martin," he said, his voice coming from far away

through the ringing in my ears, "I'm finished. You take over. I promote you to the rank of sergeant. Carry on . . ." His voice trailed off and he said something that sounded like ". . . que Dieu vous protège!" I couldn't help thinking that was all right with me because in the fix I was in I could use all the protection I could possibly get. It also occurred to me in a fleeting second that the responsibility for the outcome of the battle of Narvik now rested on me. I thought I might as well continue. Retreat was impossible. The Nazis, with their superior armament, would never let us get away alive. So what was the difference?

Pierre had escaped without a scratch. I yelled to him to keep on firing and he and a second man spelled one another in emptying their subs in the direction of the platform to prevent the enemy from getting organized. I knew the situation was hopeless. I had eight men left in battle condition and we were running short on ammunition. If it had been dark we could possibly have crept up to the platform and tried our luck with hand grenades or we could have attempted to escape down to the water. But there was no darkness—and there wouldn't be any for another six months. I had a good notion to run for my life because I saw very clearly that anything I was about to do could only end in certain death for us all but the planes saved me from committing a foolish act. I had forgotten all about them. It was now precisely 1600 hours and they were sweeping out of the clouds, dropping their bombs on the battery.

Unhappily, the contours of the mountain did not permit them to get close enough for a direct hit. Their aim was perfect but the configuration of the terrain favored the Nazis. The clusters exploded either too high or too low. The bombing had another unexpected effect, however: as soon as the planes went into action, the halftracks and artillery disappeared into the tunnel. The

Nazis had hauled them back. The platform was now deserted and I realized the only opportunity to get close to the battery had now come. I looked at Pierre and saw he was thinking the same thing. Pierre had changed noticeably. His cheeks were flushed and he seemed wide awake and eager to go into battle. I wondered whether this was the effect of the Red Cross letter. But there was no time for analysis. The planes had just disappeared into the clouds after dropping a last round of bombs.

"Take two men," I yelled at him. "We'll smoke them out. Use your eggs. I'll take the far side; you take the other!"

We climbed out of the gully. The rest of the men followed me. From the corner of my eye I saw Pierre running up the slope, crouched and supporting himself with one hand like a three-legged baboon. The other hand clutched the sub.

Pierre had reached the platform's apron and was now climbing up to the parapet. I was headed for the far side of the tunnel's mouth and needed another two or three minutes because of the distance. When I got there, Pierre was leaning against the wall next to the tunnel entrance with half-a-dozen eggs laid neatly out on the ground before him.

There wasn't much time. Quickly I removed my own grenades from the pouch attached to my belt. The Nazis could emerge at any moment now that the planes had disappeared. A rumbling noise inside indicated that the engines of the halftracks were already being started. I looked at Pierre, who then cocked his head in the direction of the hole. He had heard it too.

I waited for another couple of seconds as the sound grew louder, then nodded to Pierre and simultaneously we pulled the release wires from our grenades. I yelled and Pierre and I jumped from cover into the open and threw the eggs into the darkness of the tunnel. Explosions followed, quickly accentuated by shouting and yelling inside and we repeated the performance although the Germans had now started to shoot from inside. The shots went wild and ricocheted from the walls.

I was yelling at Pierre to get off the platform and to take cover in case they came out again but he didn't budge. He had his last two eggs in his hands and I could swear he looked at them with a loving expression. Then he pulled the wires and I started to count automatically: "One, two, three, four, five . . ." Christ, I thought, he's going to blow himself up, the bloody fool! But I must have counted too fast. Pierre took his time. At the same moment there was a sudden increase in the rumbling noise inside. One of the halftracks was coming out.

With a lightning motion and as agile as a cat, Pierre jumped in front of the approaching machine and threw both grenades, one with the right, the other with the left hand. I never knew he could use his left hand with the same ease as the right.

He threw the eggs and yelled "Jump! For Christ's sake, jump!" and we all jumped from the platform. Before we had reached firm ground a volcano erupted and the earth shook and boulders, debris, stones, and ice came crashing down the slope. A yellow flame shot from the mouth of the tunnel, followed by heavy brownish-green smoke which rolled out in a thick cloud. Pierre's eggs had hit the ammunition carried on the halftrack, which had exploded, starting a chain reaction.

This time everybody was wounded to some degree by falling debris. One man had a broken arm, another was unconscious with a cracked skull. I was bleeding and so was Pierre. He had had his front teeth knocked out. His mouth was dripping blood but he didn't seem to mind. He was high. I had never seen him in such a condition. There was enough adrenalin in his blood to keep a whole battalion going indefinitely. I knew a reaction was bound to come but for the moment he was filled with glowing satisfaction. He was elated. He had acted to avenge what the Nazis had done to his family. He had paid them back an eye for an eye. The pride made him forget everything else—at least temporarily.

Above us the tunnel was blocked by what seemed a minor rockslide. Inside there was no sound. The crews had either been shredded into small pieces by the explosions or buried alive, in which case gases and fumes would have choked them in a matter of minutes. I was inclined to think the explosions had killed them instantly but in any case the battery was neutralized. The road to Narvik was open.

We were busy for several hours taking care of the wounded. A few more died during what would have been night if it hadn't been for the midnight sun. Richard was still alive, but just barely. In the morning relief came. Another troop transport, preceded by a British destroyer sailed into the fjord. This time the battery in the mountain was silent. The colonel, after hearing Lieutenant Richard's report before he was evacuated on a stretcher, confirmed my commission. I was now a full-fledged sergeant. The troops disembarked and continued the pincer movement from the south for which we had blasted the way.

Narvik was taken, and what remained of the Nazi garrison chased into either the sea or the surrounding mountains. It was a great day for the Allies. It was also the most futile military operation ever mounted. In the end we held Narvik for three days before we retreated in a hurry. Paris had fallen while we were busy in Norway. This we learned only gradually while returning to North Africa aboard an old Norwegian freighter. We knew most of France was now occupied by the Nazis and we knew hundreds of thousands of refugees were choking the roads leading south, desperately trying to get away from the occupied zone under incessant strafing from the air by the Nazi Luftwaffe. I had no idea what had become of Maria and my son who, I was certain, were in the midst of it all.

I was depressed. My morale was low and my heart heavy when we, the survivors of the 13th Demi-Brigade, marched into the vast yard of the depot of Sidi-bel-Abbès. The sky was blue. There wasn't a single cloud. The brass buttons on the uniforms of the guard of honor glittered in the sun, contrasting with the bright red of the epaulettes. The band struck up the "Marseillaise."

The colonel marched out front, a lonely figure. Thirty feet behind him were Pierre and I, the heroes of Narvik, flanked by the tricolor and the banner of the Legion. Behind us in rows of three marched the one hundred and fifty survivors of the 13th Demi-Brigade of the Premier Régiment d'Infanterie de la Légion Etrangère.

The rest, some two thousand men, remained at the bottom of a Norwegian fjord, or strewn on the hillsides of a distant mountain.

9

Kasimir

I had been in uniform nearly two years and felt as if I had been a soldier all my life. Although in 1940 the war had theoretically ended for France, that wasn't obvious in North Africa, and especially not in Sidi-bel-Abbès where garrison life continued at a pace even more hectic than before the armistice.

For the Legion brass the war was not yet over. They didn't see eye to eye with Marshal Petain who had buckled under to Nazi pressure. The Germans had established a military commission in Oran, a scant fifty kilometers from Sidi-bel-Abbès, to supervise the slow demobilization of the French army.

The defiance to Petain and the Nazis exhibited throughout the whole hierarchy of the Legion command rocked me into a euphoric feeling of security. I found it comfortable not to think that the Nazis had been very anxious to have a word with me before I went into the Legion. I liked to think that now, with a global war on their hands, they had more important matters to attend to than chasing after me.

I was mistaken. I might have remained safe for some time, however, if it had not been for the death of K.K. which, as an unexpected side effect, reminded the Nazis that I was still around. It also put a finish to my career as a soldier.

At the outset there was no reason to assume I would be involved at all. It began a year earlier on a balmy spring evening when K.K. was urinating with great dedication standing in front of the Monument aux Morts in the barracks yard of the Sidi-bel-Abbès headquarters. The time was shortly before midnight. The stream of urine splashed lustily against the legs of a bronze soldier in the uniform of the Napoleonic period. K.K.'s bladder was well filled. He had been on a prolonged drinking spree in the Quartier Nègre. He was softly singing "Auprès de ma blonde."

The Monument aux Morts lends great dignity to the Quartier Carnot, the main depot of the garrison. Four life-sized bronze soldiers, each wearing the uniform of a different epoch illustrating the glorious past of the Legion, guard the four corners. General Rollet, the legendary Legion general, is buried in front of the monument. K.K.'s performance was of course inexcusable. He was desecrating a Legion shrine, but the gravity of the offense did not disturb him in the least. He never stopped pissing. He was dead drunk.

Corporal Castagnet, stepping softly as a cat on the prowl, emerged suddenly from the shadows into the light of the single bulb suspended above the monument. He planted himself beside K.K., who grinned when he recognized the corporal but without reducing the flow of urine. He liked the idea of having company.

"What do you think you are doing?" asked Castagnet.

"What does it look like?" said Kasimir pleasantly. His lilting speech was only slightly slurred. He saw a dark cloud pass over Castagnet's face and thought he should elaborate.

"I am pissing, Corporal. I am supplying badly needed moisture to this young tree."

"That's no tree," said Castagnet, who had no imagination. "It's a statue."

K.K. looked up and squinted. "Indeed it is," he said. "How could I have been so mistaken?"

He buttoned his fly and saluted the statue, precariously rocking back and forth on his heels. Castagnet grabbed his arm to steady him.

"Stand still," he bellowed. "Show me your pass. It's past curfew."

"No pass, Corporal," said Kasimir. "Don't need a pass."

"That's what you think," said Castagnet.

"Fuck off," said Kasimir amiably, nearly falling to the ground.

Castagnet tightened his grip.

"Come on. I'll lock you up overnight. You'll get four weeks in the slammer when the captain sees you in the morning, you drunken sonofabitch!"

"Fuck you!" said Kasimir, falling in step alongside Castagnet. They marched briskly across the yard toward the Poste de Police, the guard house. The rhythm of their steps aroused K.K.'s musical instincts. He began to sing the "Marseillaise" at the top of his lungs. A window opened and a sharp voice yelled "Shut up!" but it failed to discourage Kasimir who continued to sing.

Castagnet pushed him through the door into the guard room where the duty sergeant was sleeping on a cot. The commotion woke him immediately.

"What's up?" he asked.

"Stinking drunk," said Castagnet. "No pass. Caught him pissing on General Rollet's grave. I'll lock him up and report him in the morning to the captain."

"Fuck you, Castagnet," said Kasimir, and this time the corporal's Corsican temper boiled up. He stepped up to Kasimir, who stood grinning in the center of the room swaying like a pendulum, and raised his fist.

"One more 'Fuck you' out of you and I smash your goddamned filthy mouth, you stinking son of a whore!" he yelled. The sergeant stepped quickly between the two men.

"Stop it, Castagnet!"

"The hell I will. I'm going to teach this drunken cunt how to talk to a superior!"

The sergeant burst out laughing. He laughed so hard he had to hold his oversized belly.

"What are you laughing about?" asked Castagnet.

"Superior?" said the sergeant, who had trouble catching his breath. "Who's whose superior? Don't you know who he is?"

"I know who he is," said Castagnet hotly, "and I know what he is. A drunken asshole, that's what he is. I've had him in my section for half a year. He is a bloody fucking troublemaker!"

The sergeant threw a quick glance at Kasimir, who seemed greatly amused by the exchange in spite of his fogged-up brain. He grinned happily at the sergeant.

"Tell him, Sergeant," he said. "You're a good shit."

The sergeant now grinned too and turned to Castagnet. "How come you didn't know? Meet Lieutenant Kowalewski or Kolatchkowsky or something . . . or whatever his fucking name is . . . Koczlakowsky . . ."

"Stop joking, Sergeant," said Castagnet. "K.K. is no lieutenant."

"He sure is. His commission came through this afternoon. He used to be a captain in the Polish army. Now they have made him a lieutenant in the Legion, one rank below his old one. He is going to the front. The colonel told him this afternoon and he went straight into town to tie one on." He glanced at Kasimir, who stared back at the sergeant with glassy eyes.

"And he did a good job, too," said the sergeant. "He's sloshed to the gills. I wonder when he had the time to sew on the stripes."

K.K. was still wearing the uniform of a private. In the darkness Castagnet had not seen the two small golden stripes on the lower end of the sleeves. He stared at them now.

"I don't believe it," he said with a helpless gesture. "I don't believe it. I have been in the Legion for eighteen years and this has never happened before. It's not possible."

The sergeant shrugged. "Everything's possible in this phony war. Ne cherchez pas à comprendre!"

The corporal needed time to digest this information and to decide what to do next. Then he did what he considered proper under the circumstances. He took two steps forward and planted himself in front of K.K., who was still rocking back and forth grinning stupidly.

"I apologize, mon Lieutenant," he said briskly. "I had no idea."

Kasimir continued to grin and sway. There was no indication he had understood. But the grin changed to a pleasant smile.

"Fuck you, Castagnet," he said. "You too are a good shit!" And with that all energy went out of him; he collapsed on the sergeant's cot and was asleep before his head had touched the pillow.

I had witnessed the scene from just outside the door where I was standing guard. It happened in the brief interlude between my discharge from hospital and my departure for Narvik. The next time I met Kasimir Kolaczkowski was a year later in 1941 and the locale was again Sidi-bel-Abbès. He was still a lieutenant and in the meantime I had become a sergeant. He had just returned after a long absence and I too was just back from an extended stay in the desert. K.K. looked trim. He was wearing the ribbon of the Croix de Guerre. I saluted.

"Skip it," he said. His accent still had the languid lilt peculiar to most Slavs.

We spent the evening in his room drinking Armagnac. Kasimir had a couple of bottles of the fiery cognac, a rare commodity since the start of the war. We talked about what we had done and whether the Russians would beat the shit out of Hitler and we agreed they would. The bottle was nearly empty.

"Remember Djiri Coulibali?" he asked suddenly.

"Yes," I said. "He still owes me a wife."

"Don't count on it. He's dead. He and the whole black battalion. The Nazis never take Negro prisoners."

I thought of the tall Senegalese and his childlike smile. "What happened?"

He took a slow sip and rolled the liquid in his mouth before he answered.

"It's a long story."

It turned out that when Kasimir went to the front he was attached to the 11th regiment of the Legion, which was holding a position between the rivers Meuse and Chier south of Sedan. He commanded a company of a battalion made up entirely of Polish volunteers. During the German offensive, an armored division broke through the fortifications at Sedan but was blocked by Kasimir's unit. The Nazi advance was stalled for two weeks at the price of heavy Legion casualties.

On the evening of June 9, Captain Delaroche, Kasimir's superior, was fatally wounded and Kasimir assumed the command of the battalion. Before Delaroche died he briefed Kasimir. He told him he had strict orders to defend the position to the last man. The High Command was placing a powerful artillery unit into the sector immediately behind the Legion position. It was only a matter of hours before the heavy guns could start blazing, but until then the position had to be held at any cost.

In the morning the Nazi panzers attacked again in force. Kasimir's men stopped the advance but were pushed back to new positions in a forest of stately old trees that made it difficult for the German tanks to penetrate. All day Kasimir waited for the artillery which, according to Captain Delaroche, should have been firing for the last twelve hours. But there wasn't the sound of a single gun. The battalion had dwindled to less than half its original strength. It was therefore with great relief that he learned a battalion of Senegalese had drawn up to the lines and occupied his eastern flank. He was still hoping for artillery support.

But another day went by and still no artillery. He sent a corporal on a motorcycle on a scouting mission. The man found no sign of any artillery behind the Legion lines. As a matter of fact there was no sign of military activity for about twenty miles.

Kasimir had less than two hundred exhausted Legionnaires left and he didn't know just how much he could rely on the Senegalese. The order to hold out to the last man had not been scrapped. He scratched his head. He had no illusions about stopping the Nazis with his six or seven machine guns and the three mortars he had left. Somehow he had to increase his firepower. Kasimir remembered a friend who had fought in the Spanish republican army who once explained to him how to make a Molotov cocktail, and he knew that several drums of gasoline had been left behind by a retreating motorized unit. Kasimir sent patrols to the farmhouses in the area to collect bottles and they returned with a plentiful supply. The bottles were quickly filled with gasoline and Kasimir taught his men the trick of inserting a wick and a stopper into the necks of the bottles. He had a long talk with the commandant of the Senegalese, after which most of the bottles were turned over to the black soldiers.

Kasimir came from a long line of professional soldiers and he was a brilliant strategist. The plan he now devised to foil the Nazis was simple, so simple in fact the Germans wouldn't even have considered it a possibility. It was predicated on the fanatic punctuality of German military men. The Nazis always attacked at a certain hour. It never failed. It was Kasimir's intention to lure the German tanks into a vulnerable position where they would be helpless to defend themselves, even against a weapon as primitive as a Molotov cocktail.

The trick was to draw the tanks into a ravine that tapered down to a funnel and through which only one tank at a time could pass. He used half of the remaining contingent as bait, together with all the mortars and machine guns, by positioning them just beyond the exit of the funnel. It was a tough decision because he knew he was sacrificing these men.

As punctual as ever, the Nazi tanks emerged into the gray light of dawn, roaring through the underbrush, spewing fire and smoke. The Legionnaires let go with everything they had and the enemy responded with a vicious barrage that decimated the decoy force and silenced the mortars. But to achieve this the tanks had to converge into the area where Kasimir wanted them. They were forced to move through the ravine in single file under an umbrella of giant trees that flanked the gully. It slowed their advance.

The slowdown was the crux of Kasimir's plan. The

Senegalese were waiting in the branches, hidden under thick foliage. Kasimir was perched on a sturdy branch that jutted out horizontally and he threw the first cocktail. The bottle hit the lead tank and broke into a thousand pieces just in front of the turret. In a fraction of a second the turret was enveloped in a sheet of flame. A savage yell came from inside as the burning gasoline splashed into the face of the lookout behind the slit in the steel plates. The tank veered and crashed into a tree.

The burning tank was now blocking the column behind. This was the signal for the Senegalese. Like screaming monkeys they hurled their supply of bottles against the immobilized row of tanks and armored vehicles. Within seconds waves of flame spread across the whole line. Soldiers, some with fiercely burning uniforms, others with hair and skin afire, jumped from their stalled tanks and cars. The black men in the trees shrieked with delight.

For the moment, the Nazi advance was halted. The Polish Legionnaires, now down to forty, fell back again. At the time, Kasimir didn't know that the delay caused by the sacrifice of his men had permitted a whole division west of his own line to disengage itself from the enemy and retreat to safety. In their deaths, fewer than two hundred Legionnaires had saved the lives of several thousand French soldiers. For that action, Kasimir was given the Croix de Guerre.

Kasimir's men then retreated. The Senegalese, however, missed the boat. German patrols began to round up the black soldiers. From the protection of armored vehicles, their machine guns ticked them off one by one. They fell out of the trees like ripe plums. Elated by their fireworks and their initial surprise victory over the German panzers, the negroes forgot all elementary precaution. The German gunners never had easier targets.

"It was the end of Djiri Coulibali," said Kasimir. "He had the time of his life. I saw him. He was lying flat on a fat branch and he had his musette stuffed full with cocktails. He scored a couple of times and that got him so excited he jumped up and down like crazy. They saw him. He was hit by a machine gun—riddled by a hundred shots. They cut him in half."

The retreat continued. Neither Kasimir nor his men had any desire to fall into the hands of the Germans, who were known to shoot Polish volunteers immediately instead of making them prisoners of war. Eventually Kasimir was able to get back to Algeria and report for duty. He was sent to the Compagnie Saharienne, a corps of camel riders deep in the southern part of the Sahara desert, notorious for its murderous climate.

"Why the camel corps?" I asked.

"The colonel thought it was the best thing to do at the time. There was a good chance the Nazi commission in Oran knew of me and wanted me extradited."

I hadn't thought of that but I knew the armistice agreement with Vichy gave them the right to request extradition of anyone they wanted.

"How would they know?" I asked.

"Simple. They caught some of my men. The Nazis have ways to make prisoners talk. I am sure they have a file on me. After all I cost them plenty at Sedan. I wouldn't be surprised if they had great things in mind for me—a rope around my neck, for instance."

He was probably right. I pondered the problem for a few moments and then raised my glass.

"To Djiri Coulibali," I said.

We drank in silence.

"The colonel has changed his mind now," said Kasimir after a while. "He thinks I should get out of Algeria. It isn't safe enough for me. He's posted me to Tonkin. I'm leaving with the next convoy."

"That's the day after tomorow," I said.

"Precisely."

He filled the glasses again and we drank to his luck.

Then we drank to my luck. And then we drank until the bottle was empty.

I had forgotten that it was my turn to be the sergeant de garde the next morning. When I marched my men up to the poste de police to relieve the old guard my head was still spinning from Kasimir's Armagnac. I took over and retired into the guardhouse to rest my aching head. Nothing happened for a few hours.

At nine the colonel appeared in the distance and the sentry shouted the usual warning. The men assembled in front of the guardhouse. The colonel marched in briskly.

"Présentez armes!" I yelled, and my fifteen men in two rows executed the command in three sharp movements. It clicked like clockwork. The colonel was pleased.

"Bien," he said in my direction. I was standing rigidly at attention, my right hand raised in salute. "Carry on, Sergeant!" He turned and walked away while the bugler struck up to announce to the rest of the garrison the arrival of the regimental chief.

Nothing happened for another hour. I dozed on the cot in the guardhouse. Kasimir's Armagnac was slow getting out of my system. It was shortly before noon when the sentry called out.

"Sergeant," he shouted, "Sergeant!"

I got up, buttoned my tunic, and walked out the gate. The sentinel pointed at a man who had been talking to him. He was large, with reddish thinning hair and a protruding belly. In spite of the tropical heat, he wore a blue-striped business suit. His white collar was drenched with sweat. On the far side of the street a Citroen was parked with another civilian in the passenger seat. The car looked expensive. It was a cabriolet, forerunner of the convertible. The roof was up.

"What is it?" I asked.

The man turned to me. Two hard, pale eyes in a fleshy face. He looked at me coldly before opening his mouth.

"Sprechen sie deutsch?" he asked.

The question took me by surprise. I hoped I hadn't shown it.

"Je ne comprends pas," I said. I don't think he believed me. The majority of Legionnaires had always been of German extraction and everybody else in the corps was bound to have some rudimentary knowledge of the language if only through prolonged association. He tried again, this time in French.

"Allemand . . . allemand?" he asked. "Parlez-vous allemand . . .?"

I shook my head. "No, I don't speak German. What do you want?"

"I want to talk to Lieutenant Kolaczkowski," he said. "Kasimir Kolaczkowski."

I screwed up my forehead pretending to think. He watched my face closely.

"What's the name again?" I asked.

"Kasimir Kolaczkowski."

"He is a lieutenant?"

"Yes. Lieutenant Kasimir Kolaczkowski."

Kasimir's words of the night before flashed through my mind about the great things the Nazis had in mind for him. The man before me smelled of Gestapo. I hated to think of what they would do to him if they ever got hold of him. I had to stall for time.

I shook my head again. "Never heard of him."

He stared straight into my face. His expression said clearly he knew I was lying. He didn't trust me, but he would probably have distrusted his own mother. I could see he was furious, but he controlled himself. I don't know how high up he was in rank but no Gestapo man liked to be given the brushoff by a lowly sergeant—and a Foreign Legion sergeant to boot.

He said nothing, however, and turned back to the waiting Citroen. He climbed into the driver's seat and plunged into a prolonged conference with his partner. I decided a little investigation was in order and crossed the street. Two pairs of eyes watched me with undisguised suspicion. I smiled as pleasantly as I could.

"Is it important that you see the lieutenant?" I asked.

"Very important," said the big man.

"A personal matter, I suppose?"

He took the cue. "Yes, personal. Very personal." He hesitated for a moment as if groping for the correct words. When he spoke his tone had dropped a level. He was now going to let me in on a secret.

"It's confidential, you know. A family matter. Very important. His father sent me. I have to talk to Kasimir. It is highly personal. A great deal depends on it—money, inheritance . . . I am . . . how do you say it in French . . . the family advocate, the lawyer. You understand?"

"Yes," I said, "I understand."

Kasimir's father had been dead for many years. I remembered K.K. telling me the story at the time we shared the hospital room at Saida. I didn't need any more information. It was all very clear now.

"If that is the case," I said, "I'll send one of my men to the Bureau du Majeur. They have the files of the whole regiment there. The lieutenant is probably assigned to an out-of-town garrison. That's the reason why I didn't recognize the name but at the Bureau du Majeur they will be able to tell you."

There was a quick exchange of glances and the other man, who hadn't said a word so far, made an almost imperceptible motion with his head.

"No," said the first quickly. "Don't bother. Perhaps it isn't so important after all that we see him today. We will write him."

"Très bien," I said as I left them sitting in the car.

I walked back to the post thinking furiously. Although I had not been able to get a good look at the inside of the car I had seen a military raincoat spread out over the backseat. The heat had made the rubbery fabric very soft and pliant and it had settled around the contours of a submachine gun. The shape was clearly discernible. I had to get word to Kasimir to keep out of sight and I sent a man to his quarters. He returned after a few minutes; he couldn't find the lieutenant.

In the meantime I watched the two men. I had no doubt they were Gestapo agents. It was typical of their arrogance that they disclosed their intentions so blatantly. They were so convinced of their superiority they couldn't conceive intelligence in other people. There had been no need on their part to ask openly for Kasimir because they had come well equipped. Every time an officer passed through the gate the two stuck their heads together and seemed to compare the man with something in their hands, evidently photographs of Kasimir.

I glanced at my watch. It was now past noon. The bugler had just sounded the start of the siesta, which customarily follows the "soupe" during the hot season, when Kasimir turned the guardhouse corner. He walked toward the gate but I intercepted him, jerked to attention, and saluted.

He grinned.

"Don't be a bloody fool," he said.

"Shut up!" I said quickly. "Pretend we are talking business." He frowned for a moment and realizing I was serious raised his hand to the visor of his kepi to answer my salute.

"Don't look now," I said, "but there is a Citroen across the street with two Gestapo men in it. They have been asking for you."

He didn't change the position of his head but rolled his eyeballs in the direction of the car.

"Damn the bastards," he said. "They couldn't have waited for another day or two. I'd have been on my way to Indo-China."

He seemed to be assessing the situation in his mind for a moment and smiled. "I don't think it's serious," he said. "They don't know me, the assholes. They don't know what I look like. They have never seen me in the flesh. No need to panic, chum. Besides, I haven't got time for them. I've got to go into town. Last chance before Tonkin. Can't let the lady wait, Gestapo or no Gestapo."

And as usual he grinned.

"Don't be a hero," I said. "Stay inside the barracks. The colonel will get you out somehow. So far they don't know you're here. They are only guessing. Don't go. The moment you show your bloody face they'll recognize you. They have a whole collection of photographs."

"Fuck the photographs," he said. "Nonsense. All they probably have is a blownup passport picture. It wouldn't even look like me." He threw a quick glance in the direction of the Citroen.

"Don't go," I insisted.

"Fuck them." He was grinning again. "I'm not scared of those shitholes. Besides, as I said I have to see the lady in question or she'll screw someone else tonight and we can't have that. You understand that, chum, or don't you?"

He was already walking through the gate. "At ease, Sergeant," he called over his shoulder.

He turned the corner out into the street. The sentry presented arms. I followed Kasimir and stopped in front of the sentry's shelter painted red and green in the colors of the Legion. Kasimir marched toward the center of the town along the yellow wall that separated the barracks from the street. The two men in the car had again gone into a huddle but this time things began to move. The one who had talked to me jumped out.

"Kolaczkowski!" he shouted.

There was a slight, momentary hesitation in Kasimir's step but he continued his straight march without accelerating his pace.

The Gestapo man's hand reached into the car and reappeared with a carbine.

"Halt!" he shouted. "Halt oder ich schiesse! Stop or I'll shoot!"

Kasimir ignored him. He continued to march but he was now walking at a greater speed. He realized his predicament. There was no shelter, no place that offered protection. The street was a straight line, empty and flanked by two walls on either side. He could not turn back. His only salvation was to get out of range. He broke into a run just as the big man squeezed the trigger. The bullet hit Kasimir in the back. He stumbled and spun on his heels, his right hand going for his officer's pistol. He went down into the dust but propping himself up on his left elbow, took aim. His face was contorted in pain. He emptied the whole clip in the direction of the Gestapo agent and at least one bullet found its mark. The man dropped the rifle and staggered backwards before he collapsed.

Everything had happened so quickly I had had no time to interfere. During the shooting the other agent had jumped from his seat and slipped around the hood of the Citroen. He carried the submachine gun that I had detected earlier. Taking cover behind the radiator, he raised the snubnosed barrel but by that time I had regained my presence of mind. I grabbed the sentry's carbine which I knew was loaded. My first shot missed and went diagonally through the radiator. A jet of steam and hot water splashed out into the face of the Gestapo man and spoiled his aim. His shots went wild and whistled over my head before smashing in a crooked line into the wall. Dust and mortar came down on the sentry and me. I fired again and the second shot ripped through his throat, killing him instantly.

Kasimir was alive but very pale. He was bleeding heavily. I shouted for a stretcher and bent down to look at the wound. The bullet had been of the soft-nosed kind and had done considerable damage. When Kasimir was placed safely on the canvas of the stretcher he smiled at me.

"Thank you, my friend," he said. "Thank you from all my heart. Hope I'll be able to do the same for you some day."

Kasimir Kolaczkowski died during the night, which made me the last survivor of the incident. The big Gestapo man whom Kasimir had wounded had died too, although Kasimir's bullet had not hit any vital organ. The man would have recovered had it not been for the incredible clumsiness of an unidentified Legionnaire who, in the confusion following the shooting, accidentally stuck his bayonet into him twice while he was lying in the street.

The fact that the three protagonists were dead seemed at first sight to be a stroke of luck for the colonel. He could pretend ignorance in his report to the general commanding the region and simply put the whole thing down to a street fight between two drunken strangers and a Legion officer who had been attacked in broad daylight. The Nazi commission in Oran could hardly press for reprisals on the strength of such a report. The sentry and I were the only witnesses and there was no doubt I had acted in the line of duty. The Gestapo man had shot at me first. The bullets imbedded in the wall proved it.

Needless to say I had told the colonel the actual sequence of events and it was clear he wasn't happy. On the contrary, he was furious about the Gestapo interference but the official version he sent to the general was a smooth bit of coverup. He knew the Nazis would see the report as soon as it arrived at Oran headquarters.

There was only one flaw which the colonel had overlooked: the Nazis knew their men had not been in Sidibel-Abbès by accident but on a specific assignment. The two agents had been killed in the execution of the assignment, which would make their superiors think there had been a leak. Not knowing how stupidly the two men had given themselves away, they would want to find out how and why their cover had been blown. They also knew the colonel's story was a fabrication. They were bastards but not entirely dumb. There was bound to be an official investigation in which I would be the central figure. After all it was I who had bumped off one of their men. I would be interrogated. My background would be probed. There was no doubt in my mind that someone, somewhere, would compare notes and match bits and pieces of information and that at some point along the line the circle would close. The present would latch on to the past. Once again the Nazis were only one small step behind. Too close for comfort.

In my guts I knew my Legion days were numbered.

— 10

Madelaine

Kasimir's death triggered a second major crisis for me in a year. The first had been bad enough when I returned from Narvik and found that Maria and François had disappeared in the tidal wave of refugees that swamped the roads of France.

For two months I had been without news. I had no idea what had become of the two women and my son. I didn't know whether they were alive or dead. People who had managed to cross over to Algeria told of Nazi atrocities and of continuous bombing and strafing of the roads leading to the south, clogged by the retreating French army and by tens of thousands of refugees.

I was depressed and toying with the idea of chucking

everything and going back to France to look for them, not caring that this would be desertion. In wartime deserters are shot, but I had reached the point where I didn't care anymore.

Sergeant Bayer's therapy yanked me from my misery. He was the vaguemestre, the regimental postmaster. I had pestered him daily for weeks in hopes of getting a letter from Maria and had disrupted his men's work with my insistence that they go through the mountains of mail piled up in the office.

Bayer was experienced in the ways of the Legion. Instead of throwing me out, he correctly diagnosed my state of mind and decided to cure me. I didn't know anything about him except that he had a steady woman in town and that he had been in the Legion for many years. What I didn't know at the time was that he had been postmaster before—in the German army. One day he had received a large shipment of cash for the regimental payroll. When he saw all that beautiful money, temptation struck. He stashed the money in a suitcase, bought a civilian suit, and crossed the border into France where he headed straight for Paris and the glittering brothels of Rue Blondel. When he sobered up a few weeks later, he was broke. As soon as his befogged brain cleared sufficiently for him to realize the extent of his predicament, he signed up for a five-year stint in the Legion. Five years had stretched into twenty.

He told me the story one evening after we had drunk two bottles of the potent red wine of Algeria. Ironically, the Legion had made the embezzling ex-postmaster of twenty years earlier postmaster again. He found the coincidence a big joke.

Apart from his one-time excursion into crime, Bayer was an honest man with a simple, down-to-earth philosophy: he was convinced a man's troubles could never be so serious they wouldn't dissolve in a woman's arms.

"A good fuck cures everything," he used to say and

he decided to apply the cure to me to rid me of my depression.

Lisa was the madam of a house in the Quartier Nègre, the red light district of Sidi-bel-Abbès. She was also Bayer's fiancée. A big and husky blonde, she matched Bayer in size. He had told her about my problems before he took me to the house.

"Take care of him," he said after he had handed me over to her. "He's in bad shape." Turning on his heels he marched out of the brothel.

Lisa took me upstairs without preliminaries. When I wanted to pay she said it was on the house. "The first time only," she said. "The next time you pay."

Bayer had already told me Lisa wasn't working actively in the brothel anymore except for special customers. Apparently she had saved enough money. In two years Bayer was due for retirement, at which time they planned to get married and move to Oran where they had bought a house.

In my depressed state of mind I had forgotten how long I had been without a woman. Lisa sensed my needs. She was an artist. For the first time in many weeks my sleep was deep and undisturbed by wild dreams. In the morning my head was clear and filled with new optimism. The optimism proved justified. Three days later, while once again on guard duty, Bayer sent a man with a letter over to my guardhouse. It had been postmarked more than a month earlier and was from Maria. Just a few lines. They were alive, it said, and together in a small village in the Midi. It had taken them six weeks under the strafing bullets of the Nazi planes to reach the south of France.

As soon as I was off duty I asked for a midnight pass. Bayer and I got good and drunk in Lisa's brothel and this time she made me pay.

That had settled my first crisis. Now, a year later, there was another, although on the surface everything seemed calm and normal. Garrison life went on as usual and the colonel appeared unconcerned. I hadn't heard from him since Kasimir's death. For all I knew he may have thought the problem would go away if he ignored it. I thought it strange the Nazis hadn't moved in weeks. It wasn't their usual practice to let things get stale. It was puzzling there hadn't been an official investigation into the Kasimir affair but they may have had second thoughts. Perhaps they didn't want to advertise that the two men who went after Kasimir were Gestapo or that they were embarrassed by the clumsy way the thing had been handled. Besides, they knew the military and political situation in Algeria was not clear-cut at the time. The Nazis had a firm grip on metropolitan France and the Petain government, but in North Africa things were different. The French were militarily strong and the high command not exactly enamored of Petain. The Nazi commission in Oran knew it was on shaky grounds and that it would be unwise to provoke more incidents of the Kasimir type.

When the Nazis finally got around to me it was done "legitimately and in accordance with the stipulations of the armistice agreement relative to the extradition of persons wanted by the government of the Third Reich," to use some of their own phrasing. It was another mistake on their part because it precipitated my exit from the Legion, where I had always been a sitting duck. They would have been better off sending another Citroen, although I had been walking around with a loaded forty-five in my shirt since the day they shot Kasimir.

It was also a mistake that they forwarded the demand for my extradition through the mail. When Bayer saw the official envelope he steamed it open. He was quite adept in such matters. After he had glued it up again he came to see me and we went to Lisa's.

"What are you going to do with the letter?" I asked.
He shrugged.

114

"Give it to the colonel," he said. "In a day or two. Can't sit on it too long."

I sipped my drink, trying to sort out my thoughts.

"You've got to get out," said Bayer. "Tonight. To Oran and to a boat. It's the only way."

Lisa nodded and ripped a corner from a newspaper. She scribbled something on the white margin and slid the paper across the table.

"Go and see Madelaine in Oran. She used to work for me. She'll put you up until this thing cools down. That's her address."

"Why would she stick her neck out for me?" I asked. "She doesn't know me."

"She hates their guts," she said. "They killed her man. He was a prisoner-of-war. Shot while trying to escape, they said."

Lisa and Bayer meant well but it couldn't be done. It would place me in double jeopardy: if I bolted I would be a deserter and the French would be looking for me as well. Between the French military and the Gestapo my chances of escape would shrink to nil. It was worse than suicide. I said so to Bayer and he understood.

"Like sitting with one ass on two chairs," he said. "But what are you going to do?"

"Work through the colonel," I said. "He is in this as deep as I am. It's my only chance."

I intercepted Captain Durelle in the barracks yard, which was against regulations. In the Legion everybody goes through channels, la Voie Hièrarchic. He frowned, but when I explained the reason for my insubordination, he moved quickly. He was a veteran of the First World War and had no love for the Nazis. Less than an hour later a messenger knocked at my door in the noncom dormitory. I was to see the colonel at once.

The colonel was not a tall man but with his broad shoulders and strong neck he gave the impression of power, strengthened by black bushy eyebrows which

115

contrasted with the gray of his head. The extradition demand was on the desk before him. I could see the familiar eagle clutching the swastika in its talons, the official seal of the Nazi Reich. I hoped Bayer wasn't in trouble but the colonel did not seem interested in how I had found out the Nazis wanted me. I saw he was furious. His face was purple and the veins stuck out on his forehead. I was afraid he was going to have a stroke.

"The bastards," he said, trying to keep from shouting, "the filthy bastards. This is the first time they want a man because he did something in the line of duty and the trouble is they have every fucking right because of Petain, that senile asshole. It goes against everything I and this army stand for but they have me over a barrel. I have to hand you over. I have no choice!"

I felt my guts squirm.

He picked up the paper and read it again.

"I don't understand it," he said, shaking his head. "It doesn't make sense. They wouldn't want you because of the Kolaczkowski thing. It's all settled." He shook his head again and stared at me.

"Unless there is another reason," he added, continuing to stare. "Unless there is another reason. Well . . . is there?"

"There is, mon Colonel," I said. Then I told him about the Swiss border incident which had cost the Gestapo one man, and the kidnap attempt in Zurich which had cost them another. And then, I said, there was a small matter of being a volunteer in the enemy army instead of fighting for the glory of the Fuehrer, which in itself was good for the noose without a trial.

He listened attentively.

"That explains it," he said, turning to Durelle, who had been sitting on the window sill. They went into a low-voiced discussion.

I was standing stiffly in the center of the room, not too happy with the colonel's initial reaction. For a moment I regretted I hadn't followed Bayer's advice and taken off. At least I would have had a fighting chance. Now it looked as if I was hopelessly trapped.

I tried to control my rising panic. I knew the colonel had the reputation of being a tough sonofabitch. His regard for human life was probably nonexistent. In his years as a Legion officer he had probably sent thousands of men to their destruction—but somehow I couldn't quite see him handing a man over to the enemy on the strength of a bloody piece of paper. But then again, human nature was full of variables. The colonel had just married a twenty-five-year-old actress who had slept with more than half the officers in the garrison. Perhaps the nights with that big-breasted nymphomaniac and her demands on him had softened his brain and made him still more impervious to the troubles of others. I wondered if I shouldn't make a dash for the door.

But there was no time. The huddle was over.

"Shit on the bastards," said the colonel. "We are not extraditing you. We are kicking you out. Tonight. Now!"

He turned to Durelle.

"See he gets his papers," he barked.

"But mon Colonel . . .," said the captain, "how are we going to do that? What are we going to tell the Boches?"

"Fuck the Boches," said the colonel with conviction. "The man has to have papers. Anything will do. Fake them. Give him a dead man's papers . . . Hold it!" He paused while the wrinkles on his forehead creased deeper. "I've got an idea."

He picked up the phone.

"The hospital. Dr. Basson. On the double!"

He tapped the desk while he waited. The doctor came on.

"Jean," yelled the colonel, "have you got any dead today? Yes, dead, I said. Dead Legionnaires."

It took the doctor some time before he realized the

colonel was serious. Yes, he had one death: an old Legionnaire, retired, dead from old age and too much booze. His liver was shot. His name was Alphonse Demarais.

"Good," said the colonel. "Hold everything till you hear from me," he said and hung up.

The colonel's eyes sparkled. "Durelle," he barked again. "Splendid idea. Switch the papers. Bury the man under Martin's name. And tell the fucking Germans Martin is dead—dead and buried. His liver was no good. That'll fix it! If they don't believe it show them the grave. Make sure there is a cross on it and the name. Splendid!"

Durelle grinned broadly and strode from the room.

The colonel shook my hand. "I remember you from Narvik," he said. "You'll be all right."

I saluted and made for the door. "Démerde-toi, mon garçon," I heard him say before I closed the door behind me.

An hour later Durelle delivered the discharge papers to my room. He too shook my hand and wished me luck. The paymaster had chipped in with a couple of thousand francs, double the official demobilization allowance. There was also a bus ticket for Oran.

As far as the Legion was concerned I was now dead, but ex-Legionnaire Alphonse Demarais did not take any chances. Instead of marching through the main gate he climbed over the wall behind the kitchen building where he knew from his former life that there was an opening in the barbed wire. There was no reason to make it easy for them if they should happen to be watching the place —as they had been for Kasimir.

I avoided the main streets and made for the bus depot through dark lanes. As always there was a crowd waiting. Good. The more the better. Leaning against the wall I scrutinized the faces. If a Nazi agent was in the crowd,

I didn't spot him. No one looked suspicious. A few soldiers on leave, a few Spanish colons, husbands and wives, but mostly Arabs with bundles, live chickens, and small children.

The ride to Oran took four hours. It was almost midnight when we drove into the town. It was blacked out and the few street lights were painted blue. I remained in my seat until the bus was empty and left only after the driver had given me a questioning look. The coast seemed clear. Stepping from the bus, I turned in the direction of the harbor in the low part of the city. I needed a place to sleep. In the morning I would investigate passage opportunities.

The musette was hanging from my shoulder by a strap that bit deeply into the flesh through the thin fabric of my summer uniform. The bag was heavy; I had filled it up with tins from the kitchen on my way out. Food was rationed and I wouldn't get my coupons until I had settled somewhere.

The street was deserted but looked normal, which made me relax a little. I saw nothing unusual but I nearly ran into a woman who stepped suddenly from a laneway. I recognized her. She had been on the bus, probably the wife of a Spanish colon. She wore a sarape-type cloth over her sholuders which made her appear bulky. I tried to step around her but she grabbed my arm.

"Stop!" she said, in a deep voice.

I attempted to yank free but she hung onto my arm with amazing strength.

"To the wall," she ordered.

It wasn't a woman. It was a man in a woman's clothes. It occurred to me that their technique had vastly improved since they had shot Kasimir. The muzzle of a revolver appeared from under her wrap.

"Raise your arms!"

I obeyed.

"Drop the musette!"

The clanging of the tins on the pavement aroused his suspicion. "Push it toward me," he said. Now the German accent was unmistakable.

In my youth soccer had been my favorite sport. I was known for the power and precision of my kick, which had saved the day for my team time and again. I hadn't played soccer in years but the reflexes were still there. When I kicked the musette with my military boots it flew in an arc through the air and the heavy tins connected hard with his knees. The impact didn't do any damage but he hadn't expected it. It forced him to take a step backward and he stumbled down the curb, momentarily losing his footing. The reprieve was just long enough to let me pull the forty-five from my shirt and pump three shots into his chest. He dropped the gun and collapsed.

As I retrieved the musette a shot whistled past me so close I felt the air brush against my cheek. Behind me there was the clatter of boots and another shot. I had three more bullets in the pistol and used them all shooting in the direction of the sound. I couldn't see anyone in the darkness but there were more shots now. They missed and I picked up the musette and ran. The port was now out of the question. Their first thought would be to look for me there. In another hour they would probably have every available man out in the streets. I had to get out of circulation—fast.

I still had the scrap of paper Lisa had given me with the address of the girl who had worked for her. The address was on it but I had no idea where to find it. Light filtered through the cracks in the blinds of a bistro at a street corner I was passing. A customer was just leaving and I rushed up to him and showed him the address. He broke into a broad grin.

"That's a whorehouse, soldier," he said. "Horny eh?"

I grinned back at him and nodded.

"It's way down near the port," he said. "Quite a distance. But why go that far? I have a sister. She's got her place a couple of blocks down the street. She is pretty and won't mind picking up a little money. Come on with me!"

"Sounds great," I said, still grinning while my ears were straining to pick up any suspicious sound in the street, "but I can't. My chums are waiting for me. We've got to get back to the barracks. Sorry."

"It's a shame," he said. "She is a nice girl. Screws well too. But I know how it is; I was in the army myself. Come on, chum, I'll show you the way."

He slid his arm under my elbow in a gesture of jovial solidarity and we walked arm in arm toward the port area. He talked about his sister and how nice it would be to come and see her on my next leave. Glancing over my shoulder in near-panic, I said I would.

"Just ask for me at the place where you met me," he said. "Ask for 'Bec' Cassé. That's what they call me. My real name is Jean but they call be Bec because my beak is all smashed. My nose, you know. I used to be a boxer."

I had seen his flattened nose. It was grotesquely shaped and gave his face a lopsided look.

"Don't forget the name—Jean 'le Bec' Cassé," he said and pointed to a side street. "There you are." He shook my hand warmly and disappeared into the darkness.

The street was narrow and drab, the two-story houses unpretentious. I found the number; a single red bulb illuminated the entrance and I went in. There were only a few customers in the front room drinking beer with several half-naked girls at bare tables. I asked for Madelaine.

She came down the stairs, about forty, tall, with good legs and wearing heavy makeup. Her eyes were the best part of her face; large, gray, and clear. They reminded me of Maria's eyes. Madelaine was suspicious at first but

121

I still had the scrap of paper and she recognized Lisa's handwriting. She quickly took me upstairs to her private quarters. It wasn't safe downstairs, she said, patrols were always popping in for a drink or a quick go at one of the girls.

It had been a long day and I was exhausted. Madelaine seemed to sense it and filled a glass to the rim with brandy. While I sipped it she ran hot water in the tub of her tiny bathroom. I climbed in and she massaged my back while the warmth of the water soaked into my worn bones. Afterward she rubbed me dry and we talked for awhile. There was only one bed in her room, but as expected in her trade it was wide enough to accommodate two. By the time I went to bed my fatigue was gone, which helped me greatly to enjoy Madelaine's hospitality to the fullest. Before we finally fell asleep she said she was going to take me to the waterfront in the morning where she had many friends. She was also going to talk to an officer aboard the *Sidi Brahim,* a freighter bound for Marseilles. He was an old customer and owed her a favor or two.

The plan—as good as it was—did not materialize. At least not immediately because the town's only morning paper had my picture plastered across the front page with the inch-high caption: "Wanted Dead or Alive—Reward 10,000 francs!"

To this day I don't know how they got hold of the picture. It was a good likeness. Too good for me to get out into the street. Someone was bound to recognize me. But the picture wasn't all: they had my real name and they knew I was going under the name of a dead man. Both names were there. It meant the colonel's coverup had been blown and that he too was in trouble. Ten-thousand francs was a powerful inducement. The average Frenchman made only 600 to 800 francs a month at the time and from the way they described me it wasn't going to generate any feeling of pity in anyone who had a chance to turn me in. The story was lurid: a deserter who had stolen the papers of a dead soldier; killed a police officer without provocation and injured another; already wanted for a series of murders; a hardened criminal; armed and dangerous; to be shot on sight.

They meant business. The paper had hardly hit the street when the whole city was plastered with hundreds of hastily printed identical posters, each screaming for my capture dead or alive. By now every man, woman, and child knew my face.

Madelaine took it all calmly. "You stay here," she said, "I'll go alone and talk to my sailor friend. We'll get you down to the ship somehow after dark."

I admired her calm and wondered how much of her attitude was due to her hatred of the Nazis who had killed her lover and how much to the golden heart proverbially attributed to all whores. I still don't know why she took the risk. She had known me for just a few hours and there was a death penalty for harboring fugitives from Nazi justice.

My thoughts were cut short by a rap on the door. Madelaine was wanted on the downstairs phone. She was back after a few minutes, her face whiter than before. It was still too early in the day for makeup.

"That was a friend at police headquarters," she said. Madelaine seemed to have friends everywhere. "He is worried about me. He says they know you are here. Someone squealed. Someone who saw you come here last night."

The pimp, I thought. Jean 'le Bec' Cassé, the man who wanted to pawn off his sister on me. If she was his sister. The filthy bastard! Madelaine disappeared again. When she came back she threw a brown burnoose on the bed and a tarboosh, the tasseled red cap of the Muslim. Both had seen better days.

"Quick," she said, "put it on. We've got to get out of here." I pulled the burnoose over my uniform. It was dirty and it stank. The tarboosh didn't cover my head completely, although my hair was clipped in the style of the Legion. An Arab with blond hair sticking out from under his tarboosh was more than conspicuous and Madelaine agreed. A few gobs of brown shoe polish darkened my rudimentary sideburns. I wouldn't stand up under close scrutiny but that didn't bother me at that moment. The main thing was to get out of the brothel before the police or the Nazis came, or both.

At the door, Madelaine stopped. "Wait a moment," she said. "I've forgotten something."

She walked back to the dresser, opened a drawer, and brought out a knife. Spring blade. She depressed the catch to make sure it worked. The blade snapped up— four inches of sharp steel. The handle was bluish perlmutter. She dropped it into her purse.

"Tool of the trade," she said, smiling. "Some of the boys play rough."

It was only a short walk to the docks. There was the usual hustle and bustle of a busy port, a few uniformed police here and there. Nothing out of the ordinary. Yet something was wrong. Something did not quite fit the picture. First I couldn't put my finger on it and then I realized that there were too many idle people in the crowd, apparently loafing or walking steadily back and forth, mostly in pairs.

I was squatting Arab-style on the ground resting my back against the wall of a building, emulating Arabs who were waiting to be called for loading work. I kept at a distance, since my disguise wasn't good enough to fool them. The Gestapo men were easy to spot. I counted more than thirty. Neither their complexions nor their clothes fitted in with the character of a North African port. They had probably been brought in in a great hurry. If I hadn't been so tense I might have been amused by the thought that their prey was hardly more than an armlength away, but I shuddered when I thought of the consequences if one of them should recognize me. Dead or alive, said the poster. They wouldn't give me a chance.

Two of them walked past me so close their trousers nearly touched my knees. My suspicions were confirmed. They were talking in German. Madelaine had gone aboard the *Sidi Brahim* to find her sailor friend. The ship was moored only a few hundred feet from where I was squatting.

An hour went by and nothing happened. Some of the Arabs had been picked for work and were replaced by others and another hour passed before things began to move. A short man with a protruding stomach and a triple chin came waddling out from one of the sheds and walked down the row of squatting Arabs. He pointed at four or five and then beckoned to me.

"Get going," he said and then he marched back to the shed on his fat legs. We followed. I kept behind the others. Madelaine was nowhere in sight.

In the shed, orange crates were piled ceiling-high. The fat man said we were to load them on the *Sidi Brahim*. I began to recognize Madelaine's subtle hand. The access to the ship was roped off and patrolled by uniformed policemen. A gangplank led straight into an opening in the hull through which the crates were carried into the hold.

At the foot of the gangplank I had to pass two civilians. One, with a clipboard, kept track of the coolies entering with their load, ticking them off as they came back emptyhanded. He looked harmless. The other one looked more dangerous. When his eyes met mine the old familiar feeling of apprehension came back and automatically I shifted the crate on my shoulder a few degrees to shield my face from his stare. He had short-cropped sandy hair. His eyes were without expression, the chin jutting forward and the shoulders broad and muscular. The way he stood he could have been a big-game hunter poised to snap into action at a second's notice.

Inside the hold I had to turn sharply to the right and for a moment I saw him from the corner of my eye. He was staring at me. He may have had a dozen different reasons, none of them to do with me, but by that time my senses were already sharply honed. I felt the presence of trouble.

But nothing happened. I continued lugging crates into the hold and in the process passed the two men so often I lost count. "Clipboard" checked me off every time and the other seemed to have lost interest in me. By mid-afternoon the shed was almost empty and I lifted a crate for the last trip. As I dumped it on a pile in the hold I heard a low whistle. In the corner, hardly visible, was a ladder leading to the deck through a square in the ceiling. The opening framed the head of a man wearing a sailor cap.

"Come up," he whispered.

I climbed up to the deck. Madelaine was sitting on a coil of rope. The man with the cap was obviously her friend.

"Sit down," she said. "Keep out of sight."

I sat down next to her. "They'll miss me," I said. "They know I'm on the ship."

"Never mind," said Madelaine. "We'll fix that."

An Arab whom I hadn't seen was already climbing down the ladder. He wore a burnoose the same color as mine.

"He's taking your place," said the sailor. "He likes it because he's getting your pay and hasn't moved his ass all day." He laughed and put his arm around Madelaine's waist. She stood up brushing dust and dirt from her skirt.

"I'm going back," she said. "Gaston will look after you." She bent down and put her arms around my neck,

126

kissing me warmly on the mouth. "Bonne chance, cherie," she said after she had stopped kissing me. "Come and see me sometime after the war."

Gaston went with her and I stretched out on the planks. Resting felt good after loading orange crates for most of the day and I dozed off, for how long I don't know. A sharp voice yanked me from my dreams—the voice spoke in German.

I opened my eyes. The big-game hunter was facing me.

"Was tun sie hier?" he snarled.

I had enough presence of mind to grin apologetically while indicating with both hands I didn't understand.

He looked at me through squinting eyes and for a moment I was afraid he had recognized me. It was quite dark by now and the mixture of grime and sweat on my face coupled with the bad light must have fooled him. There is no doubt he was suspicious, but that was probably his daily bread in the Gestapo. In any event I felt slightly less tense when he spoke again, this time in bad French.

"Your name?"

"Abdul," I said, trying to sound as guttural as possible.

"What are you doing here?"

I shrugged. "Fatigué," I said. He had trouble with the word.

"What's that?" he bellowed.

"He is tired, he says," said someone in passable German. Gaston had come up from behind.

The Nazi stared at Gaston. "Get him off the ship. He is not allowed here!"

"Jawohl," said Gaston, grabbing me by the arm.

We walked down the gangplank. "Clipboard" had disappeared. The other one was leaning over the railing just above us, his head and shoulders outlined against the fading light in the sky.

"Get going," yelled Gaston for the benefit of the Gestapo man. "Next time I catch you on the boat I'll

kick you out by your bloody ass, you lazy bastard!"
Under his breath he mumbled "We sail at midnight. Be
back in time."

I heaved a deep sigh, hoping "Clipboard" hadn't tallied
his figures yet. I wondered if he was going to discover
there had been one man on the ship for whom he could
not account. If he did, would they put two and two
together? I hoped not.

Night fell quickly. For several hours I had patiently
waited, squeezed into a narrow recess between two sheds.
The dock area was deserted. Gaston had said midnight
and I wanted to wait until the last possible moment
before getting back aboard to reduce the chance of interference. My watch showed ten minutes to midnight. I
had kept in the shadows but now I moved cautiously
toward the open space where the ship was moored. I had
planned to use the heavy rope that held it to the dock
to climb aboard.

I stepped from the shadows and dashed across the
moonlit stretch. It took only a few seconds to reach the
edge of the water which was black below me when
a voice called out "Halt!"

I stopped and turned. He was right behind me and he
knocked the tarboosh from my head. His eyes showed
how delighted he was with what he saw.

"I knew it was you," he said in German. "That's why
I came back. Raise your arms quietly or I'll kill you
right here and now."

I knew he would. His index finger was on the trigger of
the Luger. With his free hand he fished a pair of hand-
cuffs from a pocket and slipped one cuff around my right
wrist. I could have swung out with my left but I knew
he would shoot at the slightest show of resistance and
I checked my reflexes. He reached for the other wrist
. . . but he never finished handcuffing me.

There was a sudden commotion behind him in the
dark and momentarily he pulled away from me. The light

was too poor to see clearly what was going on and everything happened with uncanny speed but I heard him utter a deep groan. He twisted away from me and pressed the trigger several times. At the same moment the *Sidi Brahim's* horn let out with a blast to announce she was ready to sail, drowning out the sound of the shots.

I thought I heard an outcry. Someone had been hit. But it could have been him who had cried out because he jerked his torso around in an unnatural movement just enough for me to see the handle of a knife sticking out from his back. I had seen the handle before—it was of bluish perlmutter. He raised himself up with superhuman strength but his body would not obey. It sagged and he slumped against me with his full weight throwing me off balance and together we tumbled over the edge of the dock. He was probably dead by the time he hit the water because he dropped like a stone.

My burnoose was quickly soaked and became unbearably heavy, dragging me down. I ripped it off and when I surfaced I swam toward the *Sidi Brahim* which loomed above me. Someone threw me a rope. I was still being hauled aboard when the thought struck me that the latest death would now be chalked up to me too and added to the previous casualties for which I was responsible. What's the difference, I couldn't help thinking. One more couldn't make things worse for me. But I was losing track of the total score. I only hoped Madelaine hadn't been shot because it was Madelaine's face I had seen for a fleeting moment in the scuffle, just before I went over the edge and into the water.

Gaston stuck me in the hold and gave me a dry shirt and an old pair of pants. It took him a long time to saw the cuffs off my wrist and afterward we shared a bottle of wine. My suspicion that they would credit me with the latest death seemed confirmed during the two days it took to cross the Mediterranean. The ship was ordered by radio to anchor outside the harbor of Marseilles in the Gulf of Lyons and wait for an inspection by German harbor police. Gaston said it had never happened before. It was obvious they knew I was aboard. But they took their time. For a full day the *Sidi Brahim* had been swinging around her anchor, waiting, but nothing happened. At dusk Gaston spotted the launch through his glasses. It was racing toward the ship, the swastika unfurling from its mast.

At the same time I climbed down the other side. I had stripped naked and was covered with heavy grease. My uniform, boots, and other things were in a watertight bundle strapped to my back. The water was cold and the shore about a mile away. The swim was a nightmare and time and again I was ready to quit with only a fervent wish to float down into the depths and into peaceful, soothing oblivion. Breaker after breaker washed over me, filling my mouth and nose with salt water.

Somehow I made it, I don't know how. I have no recollection. Neither do I know how long it took me and I will never know. At the time it felt like a century. But I made it. I came to, stark naked and bitterly cold, on an abandoned breakwater some three or four miles west of the port. The current had carried me off my course.

When I opened my eyes the sun was just coming up.

11

The Resistance

The tall man bowed slightly.

"My name is Henri. May I share your table?"

"Of course," I said. He took the opposite chair and I returned to my food. He ordered and we ate in silence.

130

When Henri had finished he lit a cigarette and dragged the smoke deep into his lungs.

"You are a tagged man," he said suddenly without preliminaries. "But I suppose you know that."

I looked up, startled.

"I beg your pardon?"

"You are a tagged man," he repeated. "No need to play games with me."

Less than an hour earlier I had not even known of Henri's existence. He had walked into my life in a small restaurant to which I had gone because I was told it wasn't too fussy about ration coupons. I had noticed how strangely deferential the owner had been escorting Henri across the room to where I was sitting. I wondered why he wanted to sit with me. There were several empty tables.

His remark had come out of the blue and made me uneasy. He was a stranger. One just did not trust strangers at that time. France was riddled with informers and an unguarded word could be fatal.

"I don't know what you mean," I said. He smiled and blew smoke through both nostrils. After a while he took a small piece of paper from his breast pocket. "Paul Martin," he read, dropping his voice so that he couldn't be overheard at the next table, "volunteer for the duration. Premier Etranger. Narvik. Decorated. Commissioned under fire. Wanted by Gestapo for murder and attempted murder. Quite a record." He stopped and stared at me over the rim of the paper.

I returned his stare while my mind raced. Who was he? Gestapo? Was it a trap? If it was, how was I to get out? The door was at the far end of the room, twenty-five feet away. Tables and chairs and people in between blocking my way. If he had a gun—and he probably had —I would never make it and I wasn't armed. Shit, I thought, idiot! Letting yourself get trapped!

He guessed what I was thinking.

"Take it easy," he said. "No need to panic. Think of me as a friend. I assure you I *am* a friend. As you see I know all about you. I could even tell you the name of the hotel in Marseilles where you slept after you jumped ship and what you ate for breakfast."

He glanced at the paper again.

"By the way, Colonel Gerard's trick didn't work. They didn't go for the story of your sudden death. Not after what happened in Oran. They dug up the body. Of course it wasn't yours. After that they went for the colonel but he got away in time too. He's probably with De Gaulle by now."

"Who are you?" I asked.

"It isn't important," he said. "For you I am Henri."

I realized that this strange meeting had not been accidental. Someone had engineered it. Thinking back quickly to the last few days I knew it could only have been Jean Moulat. He owned the bistro just across the street from our small house in Lavallière, a village on the banks of the Garonne, halfway between Bordeaux and Toulouse. It was him who had steered me to the restaurant.

I had arrived at Lavallière two days after landing at Marseilles. The two women and my son François were at the station when the train slowly limped in. I was cold. The tropical uniform I was wearing wasn't much protection and my face was blue. François cried when I took him. He didn't know me. He had been just three days old when I left.

Maria had found a vacant house. It was small but had two tiny bedrooms which let me resume my marital duties. "High time too," was Maria's laconic comment. We slept little that first night. She laughed and cried and laughed again and cried again while François slept soundly in his crib. She said it was the only way she could express what she felt.

132

France, at the time, was split into two zones. Lavallière was in the non-occupied part. The Nazis were nowhere in evidence, except for their troop trains which passed through the railway station on their way to the Mediterranean coast. On the surface, life in the village was peaceful but it was a deceptive calm. Under a thin veneer of complacency boiled a redhot core of hatred. Most men of military age were either prisoners-of-war or had been conscripted by the Nazis with the intelligence of the Vichy government for forced labor in German war factories, mostly in the occupied east of Europe. A number had been killed in battle.

Under the calm surface there was also bitter resentment. Food was severely rationed and farm products confiscated. Government agents roamed the farm country surrounding villages to pin down evaders. Detention camps were filled to the brim with people detained for resisting Vichy orders. Most were sent into forced labor. Hitler was desperately short of manpower.

I sensed the undercurrent of hostility and distrust on the second day in Lavallière when I went across the street for a beer at Jean Moulat's. I was still in uniform. It was impossible to buy civilian clothes: the shelves were bare.

The room was half-filled with more than a dozen men, mostly middle-aged, in animated conversation. As soon as I walked through the door the talk stopped and all heads turned in my direction. The air was heavy with suspicion.

Jean Moulat came to my table. He knew I was living across the road. He had seen me, but we had never talked before. I ordered a beer.

The silence pressed heavily on me and I felt uncomfortable under their incessant stares. I knew they wouldn't resume their talk as long as I was in the room with them. I was going to oblige and finished my beer quickly while fishing for change in my pocket. My table was near the window and through the pane I saw two gendarmes getting off their bicycles, which they leaned against the wall. They entered, and now the heads, as if on swivel sockets, veered in their direction. I was just getting up when one of the gendarmes spotted me. Tall, with broad shoulders and the nose of a vulture, he wore the stripes of a Maréchal de Logis on his sleeves, the equivalent of master sergeant.

"Hey, you!" he called out, pointing at me.

I looked at him.

"I haven't seen you before. What's your name?"

"Martin," I said. "Sergeant Martin. Premier Régiment Etranger."

"Ah, Foreign Legion," he repeated unnecessarily, and I thought I detected a shade of disgust in his voice.

Again the heads swiveled in unison and several dozen eyes stared at me but this time, unless my imagination was playing tricks, I thought the stares were less hostile than before. Whether this was due to my disclosure or to their dislike of the tall gendarme wasn't immediately clear to me.

"What are you doing here?"

"I live here. I was discharged last week."

"Why haven't you reported to me yet as you are supposed to?" he asked sharply.

I looked at the array of campaign ribbons on his tunic. The color of the ribbons had faded from age. Only one stood out in sparkling newness. The insignia of the campaign of Syria which had to be the latest addition since the short "war" in Syria had ended only a few weeks before. Wearing it cast a peculiar light on the man's mentality. Foreign Legionnaires, assisted by Free French, had chased the Nazi troops from Syria, but a number of Vichy personnel had fought alongside the Nazis against their own countrymen. When the thing was over, De Gaulle, as a concession to the Petain government, had permitted their repatriation to France instead of hanging them. The Syria ribbon told the story. The man was on the side of the Nazis. There was probably not much wrong with his soldierly skill, but as far as I could see some of the effort had been expended in the wrong cause.

His question disturbed me. He was right. I should have reported to the nearest gendarmerie post, but I had postponed the visit until I could decide whether to use my real name or hang on to Alphonse Demarais, the name under which I had been discharged. Technically he had the right to arrest me. My position was weak and I knew I had to bluff my way out of this.

He was growing impatient.

"I've asked you a question," he said sharply.

Still I didn't answer. Instead, I kept my eyes on his chest.

"What are you looking at?" he snarled.

"The Syrian ribbon," I said, touching it with my index finger. He pushed my hand away. His face had turned red. He knew the implication and so did the others. Several of the men stood up and grouped themselves around us. Moulat had an amused smile on his face. Our eyes met for a moment and he winked at me. The tall gendarme gave the room a quick circular look. The hostility in the air did not escape him.

"You are coming with me," he said, reaching for my arm. I stepped back and he missed.

"What for?" I asked.

"No questions. Just get going!"

"Sorry," I said. "I am still under the jurisdiction of the army until I have been cleared by Agen. You have no authority over me."

This wasn't true. I made it up on the spur of the moment. While it was true that I had to report to the demobilization center at Agen, it was only to get my ration coupons and whatever civilian garb they could spare. But my bluff seemed to work. I saw that he was

135

unsure of what to do next. No wonder. In the confusion of the period no one knew with certainty where army jurisdiction ended and civilian authority began.

"You can't leave the department without special permission," he said. "Agen is outside."

He was right again. Agen was in the neighboring department of Lot et Garonne and I needed a safe conduct pass from the prefecture of my own department to cross the line. Moulat came to my rescue.

"Nonsense, Albèrac," he said. "He is a soldier. He has to report to the demobilization center. It's none of your concern. Don't you see?"

Albèrac seemed baffled. He lifted his kepi and scratched his head. "I don't know," he said. "I am not so sure. He still has to come with me."

"Don't be a fool," said Moulat. "You can't do that to a soldier. He may not have as many ribbons as you but I can see he has got one anyway." Turning to me, his eyes winking again, he asked "Where did you get yours, Sergeant?"

I realized he wanted to get under Albèrac's skin. "At Narvik," I said.

Moulat was delighted. He was enjoying the game. "Albèrac," he said. "Did you hear that? He was at Narvik."

Albèrac said nothing, just looked quizzically at Moulat. I thought I should help drive home Moulat's point.

"We lost two thousand men," I said, "but we chased those Nazi bastards into the sea." My remark touched off a murmur in the room. Albèrac had understood. He was boiling but controlled himself, probably thinking there would be another day and he would get me eventually. He wasn't through with me, but for the moment it was more important for him to save face. He retreated.

"Bien," he said. "You can go to Agen. But when you come back drop in at the post for a chat."

"Sure," I said, though the prospect did not delight me. Albèrac left, followed by his colleague as someone snickered loudly. Moulat slapped me on the shoulder. I still had the change in my hand to pay for the beer but he said it was on the house and we all sat down again. Lavallière had accepted me.

It was Moulat who had sent me to the restaurant when I told him I was going to Agen. He even loaned me his bicycle for the twenty-kilometer trip and in return asked me to deliver a letter to his brother-in-law, who owned a small restaurant. And now I faced Henri across the table.

"Listen Henri," I said. "I never liked riddles. I still don't know what you're talking about. Besides, it's late and I should be on my way." Shoving back my chair I stood up, but he motioned me to sit down again. I obeyed automatically. His gesture was so full of authority that I had no other choice.

Henri was not impressed.

"You're forgetting something," he said. I looked at him questioningly.

"You are forgetting the oath of allegiance you took when you joined the army. For the duration. The war isn't over yet. You are still bound by it."

"Who are you?" I asked again.

He ignored the question. "We may have lost the first round but the war isn't over. We are still fighting."

"Who?" I asked. "Who's fighting?"

"We. The Underground. The Resistance. Call it what you will. France. The whole world."

"What has it got to do with me?"

"We want you," he said. "You are a valuable man."

"How do I know this is not a trap?"

"You don't," he said. "This is the chance you have to take."

In the next hour, Henri destroyed my doubts. Actually there was no need to tell me it was only a matter of time for the Nazis to ferret me out. Considering my record it was unlikely they would lose interest in me. I knew I was tagged, although I had tried to convince myself I would be safe in Lavallière and could hibernate there until the war was over—which was an idiotic notion. The run-in with Albèrac should have had a more sobering effect on my wishful thinking.

Henri was right. The war was not over. I had signed up for the duration and could be recalled at any time, discharge or no discharge. Besides, I wasn't so sure my discharge from the Legion was valid considering the circumstances. It was certain, however, that I was in danger and that at the moment I was alone in enemy territory. Once in the Resistance, however, I wouldn't stand alone any longer. Thousands would come to my aid if need be. It was a powerful argument. I agreed. We shook hands and drank to the new alliance.

Before Henri had a chance to brief me on the next move, the proprietor appeared at the door, motioning to him.

"Someone to see you, mon Colonel," I heard him whisper.

When he returned to the table, his face was grim.

"Trouble," he said. "We have an emergency. We need a man who speaks German. You fit perfectly." Less than twenty-fours hours later I was on my way to the emergency.

North of the town of La Roquette near the English channel, the Nazis had rounded up about three hundred Frenchmen and locked them into an old fortress prison. Whether this was in retaliation for a number of acts of sabotage in the region or for political reasons was not clear. What was clear, however, was that in previous and similar circumstances the prisoners had faced a firing squad. This was the nature of the emergency. The town was inside the zone occupied by the Nazis and in order to cross the heavily guarded demarcation line I needed a special permit. In mid-morning, after the evening with Colonel Henri, a messenger showed up at Lavallière who handed me a complete set of identity papers. I was now a native of Alsace, which explained my knowledge of German.

Traveling by train I reached the town of La Roquette the next day. The prison was three miles away in the direction of the coast. It had once been a medieval fortress, its predominant feature a wall thirty feet high and ten to fifteen feet thick in places. The Nazis had installed machine gun nests high up at every corner of the square, backed up by powerful searchlights and sentinels posted every hundred feet. Escape would be virtually impossible.

I got into town shortly after curfew. It was dark, which was good in case the Oran poster with my picture had found its way to the local kommandatur. My contact was the ticket clerk at the station. He had waited for me. We sneaked through dark alleys and lanes till we reached the back door of a hotel in the center of town. I was put up in a small basement room next to the furnace, which was fine with me because the month had turned rather chilly and I was still conditioned to the heat of North Africa. The hotel was the meeting place of the officers of the German garrison, which accounted for the fact that the owner was able to get all the coal he needed.

My mission did not allow me to stay in the cellar. Time was precious. I needed freedom of movement. I explained this to my contact. He left and returned shortly afterward with blue overalls and a visored cap with the inscription "Compagnie d'Electricité." I had now become a meter reader, which guaranteed me unmolested and free movement through the whole town.

My only problem was that I didn't have the vaguest idea of how to accomplish my mission. Henri's instructions had been lean and simple: "You've got to get them out. I rely on you." That was all he had said.

Père Lambardin was sitting in his kitchen when I entered. He too had been told I was coming. He was overjoyed and kissed me on both cheeks, garlic and all, in true French style, after which he produced a bottle of claret.

"What's at the jail?" I asked.

He shook his head. "I don't know. It's all hush-hush. I couldn't find out a thing."

Père Lambardin worked at the prison. He was a janitor, cleaning the quarters of the German officers stationed there. The Germans liked him and used to have fun with the friendly old man, who knew some German. They didn't know his eldest son had been killed in the German offensive and that two of his grandsons were prisoners in Germany. If they had known of his ferocious hatred he would not have lasted a single hour.

"Any idea why they were arrested?"

"No," he said, "it's all so secret."

"Does it look like they are going to a labor camp?"

"I don't think so," he said. "Too many old men in the bunch for that."

That was bad. Young and healthy specimens would have meant forced labor in German war plants, probably somewhere in the east. But if they were picked indiscriminately, old and young, weak and strong, it could only mean they were hostages. It also meant the firing squad.

What I had just heard made a quick decision imperative. The executions could be ordered at any moment. But I still needed to know more.

"I must have more details," I said. "I've got to know what they are planning to do and when. I can't work in the dark. Isn't there anyone who could help us?"

Lambardin shook his head.

I insisted. "There must be someone who'll talk. There must be some way. Bribery; blackmail; force?"

Lambardin shook his head again.

"A woman?"

A whole network of wrinkles suddenly spread across the old face and he grinned broadly, exposing a row of tobacco-stained teeth. He smashed his fist on the table.

"Nom de Dieu!" he shouted. "A woman! I should have thought of that!" He rushed for the door and yelled: "Georgette!"

Georgette came in and Lambardin introduced her to me. She was one of his numerous granddaughters, a pretty girl hardly twenty years old with lovely auburn hair and a fully developed body which not even the lean diet imposed by the Nazis on the French had been able to affect. The tight, low-cut blouse betrayed the shape of two young and exquisite breasts. There was intelligence in her brown eyes.

Père Lambardin explained. "One of the officers is crazy about her. A lieutenant. Wants to marry her after the war, the dirty Boche . . .!" He spit on the floor. "I told her to play along with him, you never know what it might be good for. The fellow is stationed at the prison."

There it was. The break I had hoped for. Lambardin was still talking while my brain worked on the master plan. I shut him up and told Georgette what I wanted from her. She listened attentively and after a few minutes of thinking, said she would do it.

Georgette worked quickly. Two days later a youngster came over to my hideout behind the furnace with a note from Père Lambardin. I hurried over to his place. I could see he was disturbed. The fate of the prisoners had been decided. Berlin had ordered them shot in retaliation for an act of sabotage somewhere in the occupied zone. The lieutenant had spilled the story over a second bottle of wine with Georgette.

Unfortunately, his knowledge stopped there. He did not know the exact time of the executions and I fervently hoped it would not be immediately. I needed time—two or three days at least. I had to work quickly. The job was too big for the local Underground and Henri was too far away, so I was on my own. What I needed was help from across the Channel. I knew the idea was desperate but it was the only alternative.

The small radio transmitter Henri had given me did not have enough power for the distance but I knew the answer: I had noticed the small reconnaissance aircraft that flew over the town every night after midnight. It came with the regularity of the tide. The Germans left the pilot alone, except for a few occasional AA bursts. They probably thought he couldn't see anything after dark anyway.

It was midnight when I reached the spot at the fringe of town which I had selected for the purpose, a sandy stretch alongside the riverbed. I had just pulled out the telescopic antenna of my transmitter when I heard the buzz of the plane's engine overhead. I turned the crank with all my strength to generate enough power. I was tuned in to the wavelength I had been told to use and mumbled my identification into the mike strapped to my throat. For a time that seemed an eternity there was no sound, just the crackle of static in my headphones. I kept on repeating the call words.

The plane passed over my head without any indication that the pilot had picked up the signal. It disappeared into the night.

"Damn it!" I swore. "The fucking thing hasn't enough power!"

With sweat blinding me, I increased the speed of the rotation until my arm refused to move. Suddenly the droning of the engine grew louder again. He was coming

142

back. This time he was lower than before. He began to circle and his voice broke through the static. He asked if he could land and I told him what I saw. He decided to try. Five minutes later the small single-engine plane came to a stop a few hundred feet from where I was sitting.

The pilot was a Canadian serving in the RAF. "I picked you up right from the start," he said, "but I was a little leery. Didn't know what to make of it at first. But when you started swearing I knew it was the real thing. I have a girlfriend. She's French. She swears like a truckdriver when she drives a car, just like you. The melody was familiar so I came down."

I couldn't help laughing. Rapidly I explained the situation. He didn't interrupt. I made sure he understood the hostages could be shot at any time. Speed was essential. We agreed on a rendezvous for the following night and I watched him with admiration as he cleared the treetops by inches.

He came back the next evening but this time he was not alone. A French lieutenant-colonel was with him and he had a plan of action already worked out. Exactly seventy-two hours from that night was the time fixed for the escape, he explained. Three successive waves of Allied planes were going to blast the west wall of the fortress which meant a minimum of danger for the inmates. Once the wall was breached the local Underground would take over and get the escaped prisoners out of reach of the Nazis.

I thought the plan was a sound one, considering the fix we were in. It was simple enough to promise us some success but it overlooked one crucial point: we did not know when the Nazis had scheduled the executions. It could be any day now. As much as I liked the plan, it wasn't fast enough. In three days the three-hundred hostages could be dead.

"What's holding you up?" I asked. "Why three days? Why don't you do it tomorrow night?"

"Impossible," said the Frenchman. "We are desperately short on planes and we need three squadrons and fighter protection for the mission. We just haven't got them. They have to be called back from other theaters. It takes time."

I could see the logic but a delay of three days was much too hazardous and I said so. I saw he was worried and I pressed on.

"What happens if they start shooting in the meantime?"

"Good question," he said and began pacing the hard clay of the riverbed. After a while he stopped.

"If they start shooting we'll have to improvise," he said. He didn't exactly say "improvise." He used the slang of the military which caused the image of the Legion to flick across my mind for a fraction of a moment. He said "Il faut se démerder," by which he meant they had to use their imagination and ingenuity "to get out of the shit."

I grinned and so did he when he saw it. If there was an emergency, he said, I was not to use the radio transmitter. There was a good chance my previous transmissions had been monitored by the Nazis, which may already have prompted them to change their plans, perhaps even by advancing the date of the executions. More transmissions would not only make them doubly cautious but could easily lead to my detection, which would completely scuttle the plan. Instead of using the transmitter, I was to have a bonfire going in the place where we now stood. The reconnaissance plane would be flying over the area at its accustomed time. If there was a fire, it would be assumed something unexpected had happened that made the attack imperative for the same night, in which case they would use whatever aircraft were available at the time. The attack would be launched at four in the morning, just prior to daybreak.

We shook hands and the plane took off again.

The scheme was insane. It depended on so many variables that a miracle was needed to carry it off. But I couldn't see any other solution as much as I tried to think of one. I was so wrapped up in my thoughts on the way back to town that I nearly ran into a German patrol. It would have been some fun if they had caught me with the transmitter.

Things did not go smoothly from the start. We hit a snag that threatened to jeopardize everything. Père Lambardin was to find a way of communicating with the prisoners to warn them of the plan, but it didn't work. Security had been tightened at the prison and Lambardin could not get near them. A guard had been assigned to follow him around during his chores. It didn't look good. Something was up.

The first day passed and nothing happened. The second day passed and still nothing. I breathed easier. The hiatus was bliss. Just one more day, I thought. In the evening of the second day I went back to my hole in the cellar. The weather had turned bad. Heavy, wet fog was drifting in from the Channel. I was thankful the attack wasn't scheduled till the next night.

On my way I passed Georgette and her lieutenant. She made a sign behind his back, so I let them pass and followed, keeping in the shadows. They walked slowly down the lane. The fog made it easy for me. I couldn't see them but I heard every word.

She had just asked him a question and he laughed, which seemed to make her angry. She raised her voice. In broken German she accused him of leaving her because of another woman. She said she had waited for him all day and now all he wanted was to get away from her. Who was the bitch anyway?

He laughed again and she said she was going to kill him, the other woman, and herself. She sounded as if she meant it. He laughed again but he was getting nervous.

"You are silly," he said, trying to calm her. "There is no other woman. I love you."

"You are lying. If you love me why don't you stay with me tonight as you always do?"

"I can't Georgette."

"Why not?"

"I can't tell you. Please believe me."

"So," she said indignantly, "you can't tell me. I will tell you why you can't tell me—because you are lying. Because you are cheating. You say you love me but you are now going to sleep with another woman after all I have given you. You liar! You cheating bastard! You swine! I hate you! I don't want you anymore! We're through! Do you hear me? Through! Through!"

It was a fine performance. He must have grabbed her hard because she muttered "You're hurting me!" It was his turn to be angry now and he nearly screamed. "Shut up! You're crazy! There's no other woman. I've got to get back for the execution in the morning . . . Oh dammit . . . what am I saying!"

Georgette continued teasing him to make the scene more natural but finally she let him go. When she passed me and brushed against me I couldn't resist. I grabbed her and kissed her. Her mouth was soft and willing. Too bad I hadn't time for more.

There was enough driftwood in the riverbed. I managed to build a fire big enough to be seen through the fog by the pilot and not big enough to be detected by the Nazis. He came at the usual time and I hoped he would descend far enough in spite of the fog to see the glow of the fire. He did. The plane circled three times overhead, indicating the pilot had seen the signal. Then the droning of the engine faded into the distance.

In the meantime Lambardin and his men had been busy. The fog was our enemy as well as our ally. Protected by fog and darkness the men had placed oil drums filled with gasoline at each of the wall's four corners.

Fuses were attached to the drums. When the time came the idea was to ignite the gas to show the flyers the way. In case one or more fuses refused to work, a man was assigned to each drum to throw a hand grenade into the inflammable liquid.

We hid in the woods and waited. The minute hand of my watch moved with agonizing slowness. The air was damp and cold and crept into my bones making me feel stiff. One o'clock. Three more hours. Two o'clock. Three. Three-thirty. Thirty more minutes.

I pricked my ears for a sound. The minute hand moved closer to the top. They would be coming now. I expected the sound of the planes at any moment. But there was no sound. The air remained still. A slight breeze swished through the trees and dispersed some of the fog. The men around me talked uneasily in monosyllables as the gloom spread. Something had happened.

Suddenly, out of the fog materialized a figure running toward us. I recognized one of the men who had been placed close to the wall to monitor the movements around the prison. He was panting.

I called out to him.

"They are shooting them," he yelled, sucking in air as if drowning. "They marched them out into the yard. I heard the commands. They are going to shoot them now!"

A black feeling of defeat welled up inside me. For a moment I felt drained and helpless. Shit, I thought, cheated in the last moment. Three hundred men are going to die and there's nothing I can do to stop the slaughter! And no trace of the planes.

But something had to be done. The planes would come, I had no doubt. They would be here any minute now but something had to be done to delay the shooting. A thought streaked through my mind. I had to gain time, even if it was just minutes. A single minute was precious if it delayed the fingers on the triggers. It had to be a diversionary maneuver. Something that would stop them because it was unexpected.

"A grenade," I shouted. "Get me a grenade, quick!"

Four hands reached from the depth of the camouflaging foliage, each holding a hand grenade. I took one and laid it on the ground. I loosened my belt and took it off, hoping my pants would be tight enough in the waist to stay up without the belt's support. It took me a minute to attach the grenade to the belt buckle while one of the men held a small flashlight. I told the others to stay behind and rushed out into the clearing between the woods and the wall, approaching as far as the terrain permitted. I knew it was crazy. I knew it had to be split-second timing or I would never lob another grenade.

The wall was high. I didn't think I could toss the grenade over the top unless I could come up with additional propelling power. There was only one thing to do: quickly I pulled the wire that started the thing going and remembering my days as a school athlete started spinning the dance of a whirling dervish, swinging the belt in a rapid circular motion over my head in the style of a discus thrower. The frightening part was that I had just a few seconds before being blown to bits myself and while I whirled in the dark, I counted the seconds in my head—one, two, three, four, five. When the time had come I let go and the contraption shot upwards at a tangent.

It didn't quite make it. The grenade hit the flat top of the wall and bounced into the air before exploding harmlessly. It didn't cause any damage, except for dislodging a few stones in the wall, but it disrupted whatever was going on behind the wall. I was close enough to hear shouting and the piercing voice of someone yelling commands.

I fervently hoped the surprise had been strong enough to stop the executions or delay them until the Germans had found out what prompted the fireworks. I expected them to come out through the gate at any moment and turned to run back for cover, but the machine gunner at the nearest tower chose that precise moment to let loose and I hit the ground.

And then all of a sudden I couldn't hear the staccato of the machine gun any longer because of another much stronger sound, and then I realized the sky had become loud with the thunder of an airfleet drowning out the machine gun. The men heard the planes too. The drums went up like giant flares and what was left of the fog was tinted red. The bombers couldn't miss.

And they did not miss. It was a highly professional job which lasted hardly more than five or six minutes. They swooped down on the fortress time and again and each time they did they dropped their bombs. The air vibrated around me with an endless row of explosions. After the third wave had passed, the wall was gone. Instead there was just rubble, dust, and smoke and the occasional fire. The prisoners broke out and stormed into freedom, dispersing into the night.

I returned to Lavallière at once on a bicycle one of Lambardin's men had swiped from the Nazis in the heat of the battle. It took me three days of pedaling but I preferred this to taking a train, which would probably be searched much more thoroughly after the blowing up of a prison.

Henri had news for me. I knew he was pleased but there had been complications. It wasn't hard for the Nazis to establish the role of the Underground in the affair and things became unpleasant for Père Lambardin. In addition, it turned out Georgette's boyfriend wasn't so dumb after all. He had been suspicious of me all the time and when I disappeared after the coup he reported his suspicions to his bosses. It was only a matter of time for them to connect Lambardin with the prison break. He not only had access to the place but was seen with me on several occasions. I was the prime suspect.

The old man couldn't afford taking chances. Knowing the lieutenant was bound to remember he had spilled the information about the execution date to Georgette, he shot the young Nazi in the neck and went into hiding with Georgette. I felt sorry for the mess into which I had dragged the girl. She was a lovely creature and I can still feel the softness of her lips. But the war against the Nazis was a rough game.

12
Colette

The double life I was forced to live would have been tricky in normal circumstances but in the twilight of the Nazi occupation it became more and more a magician's disappearing act with nightmarish overtones. A false step could be fatal. Henri expected me to move at a moment's notice and Albèrac, who had taken an uncomfortable interest in me, expected me to be where he could find me when the fancy struck him to see me. It was obvious he suspected me, which was probably due to his training as a policeman aggravated by his personal dislike for me.

Albèrac had the nose of a bloodhound. Besides, he had never forgiven me for the scene at Moulat's bistro which had blemished his self-image. Although his gendarmerie post was at Valenne, a town about ten miles from Lavallière, he had adopted the habit of showing up to check up on me when least expected. Henri agreed it was a nuisance but he said he was short on personnel and couldn't spare me. That the situation was dangerous for me did not faze him. The situation was dangerous for everybody, whether they were in the Resistance or not.

But I insisted on being given a suitable cover to keep Albèrac at arm's length.

Henri came up with a solution: he enrolled the services of Père Canouette, a man who had been building boats in peacetime in a small woodworking shop at Lavallière. The old man had switched to making small wooden toys when there wasn't enough lumber available for his boats. I was hired as a junior partner and sales manager, pretext enough to travel about the countryside. To make things foolproof, Henri supplied me with a safe conduct pass that bore the prefect's signature, although I doubted the prefect had ever seen the document. But it proved an excellent forgery—no one questioned its authenticity in all my travels. Even Albèrac accepted it at face value but never failed to shake his head whenever he had a chance to look at it.

For three months I had divided my time between Lavallière and St. Jean de Luc, a small fishing village on the Atlantic coast near the Spanish border. There was a strong German garrison in the latter place, at least double the number of the native population. Apparently the Nazis thought the area would be ideal for an Allied landing attempt and were taking precautions. Every inch of the coastline had been fortified.

Officially I was Captain Jacques, just out of the army and making a living as a commercial fisherman, skipper of an ancient trawler, the *Josephine*. I don't know what the French thought of me but I know the German soldiers thought I was all right because of the loads of fish I brought in from time to time, a welcome addition to their monotonous diet of tinned food and moldy Zwieback. The war had gone on too long; not even Hitler's Wehrmacht was eating well any longer.

Josephine was moored to the dock one day when a messenger came. He was the liaison man between Henri and St. Jean de Luc, which happened to be the last link of *le tuyau*, the pipeline, that reached from Paris to

151

the Spanish border and through which the Underground spirited people out of the country. It was my job to stash these people away in the hold of *Josephine,* which was big enough for a ton of fish, and ferry them across the Bay of Biscay to a deserted spot between San Sebastian and Bilbao in Spain, where someone else took charge of them. After dropping them off we always stayed out on the water until we had a good catch, as an alibi for our absence. The major portion of the fish always went to the Nazi garrison, the rest to the natives. I felt sorry for each fish I turned over to the Nazis but it was good insurance.

The messenger said there wasn't going to be a "shipment" this time. Something special had come up, some kind of an emergency and I was to report to the colonel as quickly as possible. This would not be easy because Henri was holed up at the far side of Toulouse while I was some 150 miles down the coast below Biarritz. Besides, I had to cross the demarcation line—which was never a pleasure.

I went to see the chief of the Kommandatur and told him I needed a replacement part for *Josephine*'s engine which I could find only in Toulouse and without too many questions he signed a laissez-passer. He was thinking of the fresh fish I delivered for the officers' mess.

A day later I stood facing Henri.

"Colette is in trouble," he said simply. "You've got to get her out."

"Why don't you just send her down to St. Jean?" I asked with annoyance, thinking of the 150 miles I had traveled on a bicycle whose stone-hard saddle had nearly ripped my crotch to shreds.

"She refuses. She isn't ready, she says. Some unfinished business. I don't know what she means and she isn't telling."

I had a good idea of what she meant but I kept it to myself.

"Besides, she says if she has to go she is going only with you. She doesn't trust anyone else."

I could understand that too. Colette was no ordinary woman. She was a myth. The French thought of her as a reincarnation of Joan of Arc. She was beautiful and soft and desirable, with all the qualities expected in a French woman. In spite of her softness and loveliness she had killed more than a hundred of Germany's most promising officers—and she had killed them in cold blood.

I had met her for the first time a few months earlier. Henri had sent me on a rescue mission to a small town in the Calvados, across the demarcation line, where she worked in a bookstore. The town, near the Channel, had a substantial German garrison. I went there with three other men because Henri had been tipped off that the Gestapo had located Colette and was setting up a trap for her. I had gone to the bookstore pretending to be a customer.

She was stubborn. She just smiled when I told her Henri had ordered her to get out.

"Nonsense," was all she said to me at the time.

My local contact reported that she was after a young major, a Nazi war hero with a chestful of medals who had just been transferred from the Russian front for a rest in the quiet of occupation duty. He was crazy about her. The contact also knew the place where the two usually met, which seemed like a lucky break for us but caused me second thoughts the more I turned the whole thing over in my mind. There was a catch: if we were so well informed it was a sure bet the other side knew as much as we did, perhaps a little more. I had a hunch it was a trap and the major was the bait, whether he was aware of it or not.

My suspicions had been confirmed almost immediately. We had been keeping the meeting place under observation, a small hunting cottage some three or four miles from town and hidden in a densely wooded area. On the second day one of my men reported that a Gestapo car was sitting in a clearing about fifteen hundred yards from the lodge, skilfully camouflaged. The vehicle was full of electrical apparatus, including several high-powered reflectors. It wasn't hard to guess what they were planning to do. Earlier in the day I had pressured Colette and threatened to take her by force if she refused to cooperate but she had asked for one more day—which was all I needed to know. As soon as darkness fell, I and my three helpers sneaked up to the lodge and hid in the bushes.

Our timing could not have been better. Hardly five minutes later a car drove up, six uniformed men jumped out, and the car sped off. They disappeared into a woodshed near the building.

Half an hour later the headlights of another car flickered through the trees. The major and Colette. They went inside. A light went on behind the curtains. We waited and so did the others. A short time later the light inside was dimmed. The Gestapo contingent emerged stealthily from the shed. All of a sudden the front of the lodge was bathed in brilliant light. The spotlights and reflectors had been mounted in a half circle on several trees cleverly hidden by the foliage.

Simultaneous with the switching on of the beams the six men advanced to the door but before they reached it it was flung open, and there, in the white glare stood the major, temporarily blinded and stark naked. He had a hunting rifle in his hand and started firing. He must have thought he was still on the Russian front.

This spoiled the whole thing for the Gestapo boys. It wasn't included in their plans. They were after Colette and the major's heroic action hadn't even been considered a possibilty. Momentarily their advance came to a halt, which cost one of their men his life. He was hit and fell to the ground. The man next to him pulled out his pistol and in turn shot the major, which was my cue to open up from behind the trees with my short-barreled sub. They were so stunned they didn't move. In the glaring light of the reflectors it was like a shooting gallery. Within seconds all five were dead.

I didn't give Colette time to get dressed. Naked, she grabbed her clothes and we ran through the bush to the halftrack in the clearing. At daybreak we took refuge in a farmhouse near Bordeaux that was owned by a Resistance member and where Colette told me the reason for her burning hatred.

Her real name was Marie-Monique, which brought another Maria into my life, I thought. Colette was her nom de guerre. Her father had been a wealthy wine merchant at Bordeaux and had given her the best education money could buy. When the Nazis came, the family's mansion was requisitioned and the commander of the occupation troops, a lieutenant-colonel, moved in. The family was relegated to the servants' cottage. A few weeks later the father was caught in the act of trying to transport a Jewish business friend who had escaped from Paris to the Spanish border. The commander had ordered him shot in public in full sight of the population, thinking this would be a good deterrent and teach the French a lesson. Mother and daughter were repeatedly raped by several soldiers, after which the mother had been transported to an unknown destination. In the confusion, Colette managed to escape.

When she told me the story she skipped over the first few weeks of her disappearance. She didn't remember what happened in what must have been a period of searing agony. She suffered a complete mental blackout, a charitable kind of amnesia that saved her from snapping into insanity. Yet a dramatic transformation occurred in those weeks. She said she didn't know how it came about (or she didn't want to tell) but it is a fact that the shy young girl who had just a short time before graduated from her convent school, emerged a sophisticated charming woman and took a job in a bookshop in a town of 50,000 to the north of the demarcation line. The town, an important railway junction, had a large German garrison, and the shop carried German magazines and newspapers.

The news spread of the pretty girl at the bookshop. Sales increased visibly. The majority of the young women in town would not fraternize with the Nazi soldiers but Colette appeared interested and approachable. She dated often—but only officers.

Soon afterward, the German commander was faced with a strange situation. A large number of his officers were disappearing without leaving a trace. Several others had been found dead in circumstances which pointed to suicide. But the commander was doubtful. There were too many of them. He sensed something was leading to the decimation of his officer corps but he couldn't put his finger on it so he called in the Gestapo. It took the professional bloodhounds only a short time to establish the common denominator in all cases—Colette. But she outguessed the Gestapo. When they came for her she was gone.

After that she worked in Paris and in Lille, in Lyon, Marseilles, and Grenoble. Each time a bookshop was her base. It provided the best yield of the kind of men she was after. She killed without mercy and without a second thought.

Her luck was uncanny. She had remained unmolested for a long time, but now the enemy had become thoroughly familiar with the unvarying pattern of her operation and had thrown out a net for her which was growing tighter by the day. At that point Henri decided to put an end to it and that was when I entered the picture.

This time I found her in Bordeaux, her home town. Although I knew she liked me, she wasn't pleased when she saw me, knowing it was Henri's idea that I was there. But she kissed me all the same. I told her what Henri wanted her to do and she thought about it for a long time. "All right," she said finally, "I'll go with you. But not right away. There is something I've got to do first."

When she told me what it was I knew there was no power on earth strong enough to prevent her, short of locking her up in chains. I thought it would speed up things if I played along and even helped her. I said so, and she promised to go with me when it was over.

The war had been good to the lieutenant-colonel who had killed her father. He was not a lieutenant-colonel any longer; he had been promoted to general. The way she had planned to approach him was so simple it bordered on the obvious. Only a woman of Colette's skill and daring could succeed in it. She knew the general was in the habit of having his dinner in the old-fashioned splendor of the Grand Hotel in the center of Bordeaux.

Her timing was perfect. When he stepped from his staff car in front of the hotel's entrance, an attractive young woman crossed his path. She stopped momentarily, stumbled, and would have fallen to the pavement if he had not caught her in time. His arm went around her waist. She smiled at him and he saw a pale and beautiful face under a crown of golden hair. A soft green dress clinging to every line emphasized a young and full body.

"Are you all right?" he asked politely. "Can I do anything for you?"

"No thank you, Excellency," she replied in German.

"Are you sick, mein Fraeulein?" he asked.

She shook her head. His arm was still around her waist and he felt the warmth of her flesh.

"No," she said, with an embarrassed smile. "Not sick . . . just . . . oh . . . it's nothing. It's too silly."

"Well," he said. "What is it?"

She hesitated and then with a sudden effort added, "It's just that I am hungry. It's silly, mon Général. You won't believe it but someone picked my purse and stole all my ration coupons. I haven't eaten in two days."

She had arrived at the point of no return. If he saw through the contrived story all was lost. Everything pivoted on those next few seconds. She saw he was weighing her words. The story had a phony ring to it but these things do happen. Purses get picked. Ration coupons get stolen. It *was* possible. He was trying to cut through his doubt and she looked up to him again and he saw her liquid brown eyes an¹ the delicate shape of her full breasts exposed by a low décolletée. Still holding her close, the warmth of her body got through to him. A sudden delightful surge sweeping through his body obliterated the caution.

"Hungry?" he said. "Well, that's no problem. Would you please be my honored guest, mein Fraeulein? I was going to have dinner alone but you would be charming company."

Colette smiled. The critical moment had passed. During the meal she played up to him and the wine did the rest. It was to Colette's family mansion that he took her afterward, but that too had been anticipated. The night was dark and the city blacked out. The general, who had eyes only for Colette, did not see us as we waited in the dark.

The chauffeur was no match for us, nor was the sentry at the gate. My men were experienced in such matters. I took the wheel as the general and Colette emerged and we drove to the woods outside the city. The general, pleasantly inebriated and occupied with Colette, hadn't noticed anything. Reality dawned on him only as he was being dragged from the car and tied to a tree. In the uncertain rays of the dimmed headlights the general stared at Colette and in one scorching flash realized he had allowed himself to be trapped like a mindless idiot.

"You are Colette," he said flatly.

She nodded and took a small snub-nosed revolver from her purse.

"You are going to kill me," he said.

She nodded again.

"But why me?"

"Don't you remember, mon Général?"

He shook his head.

"Think back. Three years."

He did not answer.

"Bad memory, mon Général. Think back to 1940. You had my father shot and you murdered my mother. You are still living in my house. Do you remember now?"

He was unable to speak. Only his Adam's apple jerked spasmodically.

Colette stepped closer to him. He screamed. "No . . . don't! Don't kill me! Please . . . don't . . . don't!"

She shot him in the stomach with clinical precision, carefully avoiding any vital organs. She wanted him to die slowly. He groaned and tore feebly at the ropes. Then drained, his body sagged, but the ties held him firmly against the tree. For the rest of the night and most of the following day she sat immobile on a rock facing the tree, watching him die. When it was over she rose and stared into the dead man's face. Then, her expression impassive, she turned slowly and joined my men, who were to take her to St. Jean de Luc. I wasn't going with her. It was better to split up. Besides, I had to prepare *Josephine* and make sure there were no complications. The general's death was going to shake every Nazi garrison in the region with the force of an earthquake. It was safer for Colette to come aboard at the last possible moment to reduce the risk of being spotted.

The fog was getting thicker by the minute and I didn't like it. What's the matter with me, I thought. Am I jinxed? The bloody fog is following me like a curse.

If the fog was getting worse the Nazis would wonder why I insisted on sailing in hazardous weather, and even if they didn't become suspicious I was going to have a tough time at the Spanish side. It was tricky enough to get through the craggy cliffs in broad daylight and calm weather, let alone in dense fog and four-foot waves. I saw a rough night ahead of me but the cargo justified the risk. I couldn't let them get their hands on Colette.

The engine idled slowly. *Josephine* heaved occasionally in response to the choppy waves that spilled over the walkway. The deck was wet and slippery. Jules was fiddling with the controls of the engine.

"When's she coming?" he asked. "We can't stall much longer. The Boches will get suspicious. We should have gone before the fog came in."

Jules was right. But he knew as well as I that we had to wait. I peered out into the sea. I didn't like what I saw.

"Fog's getting worse," said Jules. "They'll ask questions. They know we can't sail in such fucking weather."

Footsteps on the dock at last—but not what I had hoped for. Military boots. Jules looked at me questioningly.

"Get busy," I hissed. He bent over the engine, monkey wrench in hand.

They trotted out of the swirling fog, six steel-helmeted soldiers with fixed bayonets. An officer came up from behind. At first I couldn't make out his face.

"Was machen sie hier?" he asked. I answered in broken German. "Engine is acting up. We are fixing it." Turning to Jules I said "How much longer?"

"Almost done," he said, tightening a nut and looking very professional, his hands dripping oil.

The officer stepped from the dock down onto the deck. His men's guns covered him. I knew every officer in the garrison but this one I had never seen before. As soon as I saw the SS insignia on his tunic collar

I knew something was up. The SS had never been here as far as I could remember. Just the regular army. Colette, I thought. It could only be because of her. The ripple of the earthquake had reached St. Jean de Luc uncomfortably quickly.

The Nazi turned to me. "Papers?"

I handed him the Erlaubnisschein, the permit, issued by the Kommandatur. He studied it carefully before handing it back to me. Then he climbed back up on the dock. The fog swallowed the group in a matter of seconds.

As if on cue, Colette suddenly materialized, still wearing the soft green dress that was never designed for a voyage in a smelly trawler. Neither were her high-heel satin pumps. But she was aboard at last and we could be on our way.

Antoine, the third crew member, quickly untied the boat and Jules took the wheel. The *Josephine* moved slowly toward the opening of the breakwater, whose contours were barely visible in the thickening fog. We reached the gap. Ordinarily we would slow down to permit the German sentry to identify us, which was merely a formality since all the sentries knew us well. But tonight things were different. A flare, painting a crimson circle into the wall of fog, stopped us.

Jules brought *Josephine* to the edge of the breakwater and I threw out the rope, which was grabbed by someone whom I couldn't see in the blinding glare. But I could make out the shadows of three or four more people where there was usually only one sentry. The officer who now stepped into my field of vision was unknown to me too. He was SS and asked to see my papers. Christ, I thought, they are out in force tonight. My stomach was queasy, thinking of Colette down there in the cabin.

Antoine had sidled up to one of the oblong boxes built into the railing in which we kept spare ropes and

161

nets. He had the lid halfway propped up so that he could grab the submachine gun that was hidden under a layer of netting if there was need. Antoine was the best shot I ever met. He could shoot the legs out from under a fly. I only hoped he would be quick enough, although the element of surprise was on our side. The gun was good for up to a hundred shots a minute but with these bastards one never knew. They could blow us sky-high before Antoine had a chance of getting his finger on the trigger.

But the SS man was satisfied with my papers. He had probably been told beforehand we were harmless. It was just a show to let everybody know it was healthy to toe the line.

"Bad night," he said in an unexpected exhibition of civility.

"I've seen worse," I said. "Should be all right tomorrow. Fog usually clears at dawn."

He brought up his hand for a salute but apparently finding it beneath his dignity as an SS officer, checked the hand in mid-air. Instead, he mumbled "Heil Hitler," and jumped back onto the breakwater.

At last we were in open water; I felt it because of *Josephine*'s sway. The fog was thick, viscous, a wet blanket that enveloped everything with a touch of ice. I couldn't even see the stern from where I was standing. The swells became more massive the farther out we went despite the absence of wind. The darkness was eery. Normally I needed less than a day for the crossing, which included all the deceptive maneuvers I had to go through to fool the enemy. *Josephine* was a fast boat. The engine had been souped up and she moved like a dolphin. But now Jules allowed her to slow down to avoid being swamped. Every time the bow dipped into a wave, a curtain of spray rolled over the deck. I made my way through the wet fog to the cabin and looked in. Colette was sound asleep on the cot, wrapped in my blanket and coiled up like a snake.

Jules was dripping from head to toe. We checked the course. *Josephine* still had to head out into the Atlantic for a good stretch before we could veer south to hit the landing spot in Spain. Our only navigational aid was an ancient compass, a relic of the First World War. I hoped it was still accurate.

The going was slow but Jules said there was no cause for worry. If we couldn't move faster because of the fog, the Nazis couldn't either if they decided to come after us. That sounded logical enough. Jules had been a prisoner-of-war in a Nazi camp but had outsmarted his captors and escaped. He claimed he had studied their mentality.

"They've no reason to come after us," he said with conviction. "They have written us off. Just show them a piece of paper with a stamp and a signature on it and they're happy. We have such a paper and they saw it. Believe me we are in the clear. They have no brains. They are like a machine. Robots. You punch a button and they move. You punch another button and they stop. I know them. I had my fill of them in the camp. Cochons!" He spat over the side of the boat.

I hoped his analysis was accurate but I was uneasy just the same. We were not dealing with the chaff anymore but the SS, Hitler's élite, assumed to be on a much higher intelligence level than the rest—and deadlier too.

Nothing happened in the next few hours. We kept on plowing slowly through the fog. Too slow for the way I felt. Gradually the blackness of night lifted and dawn revealed the lines of *Josephine*. The sea was still rough. Two more hours and we would change course.

I had no warning that they had caught up to us. Their position lights had been extinguished and I hadn't heard a thing because of *Josephine's* noisy engine. The first indication things were not as I thought was when there was the sound of a cannon and a splash just ahead of the bow, a sound which not even *Josephine's* engine could mask.

Josephine shuddered from bow to stern. "Christ," was all I could say. "Those fucking bastards!"

Automatically Jules slowed the engine. After a few minutes we came to a full stop, heaving in the swells, the engine continuing to idle just in case. In the sudden silence their craft came out of the fog and glided smoothly alongside us. I wondered how they had found us. Radar possibly. But that wasn't important now. What was important was the sudden realization that the pipeline was blown. There had been a leak. Someone had cracked and told them about Colette and I and the *Josephine*.

Their boat was bigger than ours and loomed much higher in the fog. A powerful searchlight came on, trained on us and bathing the deck in a white brilliance. A rope snaked down and was wound around a post by Jules. Several figures climbed down. Silhouetted against the light I counted three soldiers, carbines in hand, taking positions behind Jules who had returned to the wheel. Antoine, who had been dozing in a protected corner, now stood up. The fourth Nazi, evidently in charge of the boarding party, came toward me. He stuck the beam of a flashlight into my face.

"Aha," he said, as if to satisfy himself I was the man he was looking for. I recognized him by his voice as the SS officer who had checked my papers back at the dock at St. Jean. I grinned at him as friendly as I was able to and hauled the Erlaubnisschein from my inside pocket.

But that wasn't what he had come for. The beam of the flashlight described a slow circle, taking in every part of the deck. He explored every plank, inch by inch. He did not notice the cabin door immediately because we had it camouflaged with a whole mess of ropes and nets. Finally, the beam caught the door's outline.

"Aha," he said again. "What's in there?"

"Nothing of importance," I said. "Just a bunk to stretch out on and have a glass of Schnaps."

He disliked the way I pronounced "Schnaps." I could see the flicker of annoyance around his mouth. He walked toward the cabin and I followed him. Antoine was again standing by his box. The Nazi opened the door and looked inside. I froze—but nothing happened! The cabin appeared empty. No sign of Colette. He slammed the door shut with a grunt. I breathed with relief. He walked back to the stern, the flashlight beam still preceding him. In another minute the invasion would be over and we would again be on our way.

But the prospect was too good to be true. Something caught his attention, something that had escaped him before because it had been lying in the shadow cast by the coil of rope. But now, approached from a different angle, it was in plain sight of the beam: A woman's heel. Green, scraped, and broken, but unmistakably a woman's heel.

My guts tightened into a knot as hard as concrete. I hadn't the slightest idea what to say if he should ask for an explanation.

He never did. He had his revolver out with a lightning sweep of his hand. Slamming me viciously against the railing, making me nearly go overboard backwards, he stormed to the cabin and ripped open the door. Recovering my balance I ran after him.

The door was too low for his bulk. He stooped and eased himself through the narrow frame for the three steps down. I looked through the space left between his head and the frame. Colette was standing in front of the bunk fully outlined against the light of the kerosene lamp behind her. She was naked.

He saw her. The beam of his light caught the whiteness of her skin contrasting sharply with the deep red of the nipples on her superbly shaped breasts. Her pubic hair shimmered like a golden triangle in the strong beam.

He froze. This was not what he had expected. For a fraction of a second he hesitated before leveling his gun at her, but the brief respite was sufficient for Colette. She emptied the clip of her snub-nosed revolver into his belly and chest.

The others on the deck of their boat seemed stunned at first but then I heard a shouted command. Antoine heard it too and with catlike speed snatched the sub from the box. His first shots mowed down the three soldiers like bowling pins and his next round shattered the searchlight.

Jules had flattened himself out on the planks as soon as Antoine went into action. Now he slashed the rope that held us captive, jumped back to the wheel, and opened the throttle. With a mighty roar *Josephine* took off into the waves.

The dead officer was heavy. It was difficult getting him into the water but *Josephine* gave me a hand. When she hit a wave at full speed the deck slanted nearly forty-five degrees. One kick was enough and he splashed into the water.

I groped my way back to the cabin. Colette was sitting on the swaying cot. When she saw me she rose and I put my arms around her. She was trembling. Gently I forced her to lie down and covered her with a heavy blanket. After a while she stopped trembling. I reached for the lamp, turned down the wick, and tip-toed back on deck to relieve Jules. We still had a long way to go and the Nazis were still too close for comfort.

13
The Bridge

There was no end in sight to the war. Although too many easy victories had made the Nazis complacent, they held the occupied part of France in a merciless grip. France was hungry. The huge Nazi army, like a giant swarm of locusts, devoured everything in sight.

On the surface the country was calm, a condition interrupted occasionally by local eruptions of resistance, which the few one-page newspapers still allowed to publish were not permitted to mention. The suppression of news was intended to keep the French ignorant of what was going on in their own country. As an unexpected side effect it kept the mass of Nazi soldiers in France ignorant too and lulled them into a false sense of security.

But on November 8, 1942, the pleasant calm was shattered. Allied forces under General Eisenhower landed in North Africa, an unexpected move which shocked the Nazis from their happy state of smug contentment. For a moment they were stunned.

I had been sitting in the cellar of our small house at Lavallière since the early morning, ears glued to the short-wave receiver. Reception was bad, just a high-pitched whine and the crackle of static obscuring most of the transmissions. With a roof antenna the sound would have come through loud and clear but an aerial was out of the question. The mere possession of a short-wave radio was punishable by death. High treason.

Listening for hours to the flow of bulletins beamed at the continent by the BBC in London, I had lost all sense of time. My stomach was telling me it was almost noon,

167

however, when I had a visitor. To be exact, I had two visitors in succession. The first was an old man who did occasional work at the local post office where among other things the village's telephone switchboard was located. He lived just up the street and we had had an occasional glass of beer together at Jean Moulat's.

He stayed just long enough to tell me that when manning the switchboard he had inadvertently listened in on a conversation Maréchal de Logis Albèrac, the local gendarmerie commander, had had with someone at the Prefecture in Montauban. Albèrac, worried by the political and military events of the previous twenty-four hours, had asked for permission to round up known suspects in the territory under his jurisdiction. My name had come up in the conversation, together with those of several others of the community.

"Did they say he could go ahead?" I asked.

The old man shook his head. "No. Not yet anyway. The fellow at the other end said he was going to talk to the Prefect and told Albèrac to stand by for instructions. The Prefect was expected at any time."

"When was that?" I asked.

"Just a few minutes ago. I came right over to your place," said the old man, who then left.

In a way I had expected something of the kind to happen. It stood to reason that the government at Vichy, unnerved by the new twist in North Africa, would want to have all possible security risks behind barbed wire and it was also obvious that Albèrac, an egomaniac and ambitious, would want to get into the act. I knew he hadn't forgotten me. I was not surprised to be on his list. The news meant I had to go into hiding. I didn't like the idea but I was prepared for this contingency. What bothered me was the thought that I had to leave the women and my son behind. However, I knew that at least up to that point the families of the men who had gone into hiding had not been molested. On the contrary, the wives or sweethearts were just watched, with the assumption that sooner or later the fugitive would try to get in touch with them. The scheme had worked in some cases. It was a slim sort of consolation, but consolation all the same.

Before I had a chance to collect my things for the getaway, the second visitor arrived. I had never seen him before. He leaned his bicycle casually against the wall and fished a soiled piece of paper from his pants pocket. There were only a few penciled words on the paper, an address of a place that I vaguely knew some 120 kilometers to the southeast, and the laconic postscript: "Bring the cigars." It was signed "Henri."

I wondered whether this had any connection with the new situation in North Africa. It was reasonable to assume the Nazis would rush down to the Mediterranean coast in a big hurry to get there before Eisenhower had a chance to land somewhere near Marseilles. I knew Henri wouldn't want to miss the opportunity to play a few tricks on the Nazis. I couldn't help smiling. What we called "cigars" were actually small, brownish sticks of a powerful explosive in the shape of a cigar. Henri had given them to me some time before, together with a flat, wooden cigar box into which they just fitted. Ten of them. The thought they would be needed elated me.

But the elation did not last.

"Your brother is dead," the visitor said without any preliminaries. "Shot!"

My heart missed a beat and I took a deep breath. I knew he had been caught a short time earlier and shipped to a concentration camp notorious for its low survival figures. I had been afraid for him ever since I heard he was captured.

"Shot while trying to escape," came the additional information.

"When?" I asked.

He shrugged. "Two weeks ago. Maybe three. What's the difference? We didn't know until last night."

He mounted the bicycle and rode off. For a few seconds I didn't move. Two weeks ago. Maybe three. What difference did it make? No difference at all anymore. He was dead. Suddenly, I felt sick. Bile and hatred swept through me. I felt tears in my eyes which in a helpless rage I couldn't control. I swallowed hard to regain composure.

I couldn't fool Maria. I always suspected she had the gift of extrasensory perception. She had a way of answering questions even before I had asked them. Now she looked at me and I knew she was reading my mind.

"Your brother," she said gently. It was a statement, not a question.

I nodded.

There was no more time to be lost. I blocked the pain from my mind to get ready for what I had to do. The toolbox was in its regular hiding place under the chicken coop in the small backyard. It was an ordinary metal toolbox of the kind used by mechanics or carpenters all over the world and there were tools in it all right. But under the false bottom, in a bed of soft cotton was the wooden box with the ten cigars. I had been told each one could immobilize a thirty-ton tank or a railway car.

I kissed Maria and ran upstairs for a last look at my small son sleeping soundly in his crib.

A few hours later, evening had set in as I stood on the platform of the railway station waiting for the train that was to take me to my rendezvous with Henri. I had changed into the bulky blue overalls and black beret of the French workingman. The toolbox, resting on the ground beside my feet, added authenticity to my disguise.

The train was late and I was just rolling my third cigarette when it finally steamed into the station's large covered hall. But there was something wrong. It wasn't the scheduled passenger train. It was a German troop train.

As I had feared, the German command had suspended all civilian traffic as soon as the Allied landing in Africa had become known, to clear the trunk lines for military use. All day their troop carriers had been rolling south toward Marseilles and the Mediterranean coast facing North Africa in expectation of an invasion across the water. I noticed immediately that it wasn't an ordinary troop train. It was much longer than ordinary. Through the windows I saw soldiers jammed in like sardines in a can. The number of cars indicated a regiment in full battle strength, two thousand men, perhaps more. But they were not regular army. The skull and bones insignia on their helmets could not be mistaken! it was a regiment of the Waffen SS, the professional, highly trained assassins of the Third Reich. Adolf Hitler's pets. His élite guard.

The blood rushed to my head and pounded against my skull. My brother's face flashed momentarily across my eyes, my only brother whom they had killed in cold blood. "Shot while trying to escape." A man who had never hurt anyone or anything.

I stirred and stubbed my toe on something hard and unyielding. The toolbox. The sharp pain brought me back to reality. For a moment I had forgotten the box and what it contained but in that fraction of a second my mind had formulated a plan. Suddenly, I knew what I had to do. The blueprint was there waiting to be implemented.

The train had noisily come to a standstill. The engine blew white steam into the chilly air of the station. No one descended from the cars except a handful of officers who clustered in a group a few feet from where I stood. They talked loudly and I understood every word they said. I hoped I wasn't too conspicuous standing there but they paid no attention to me. It gave me a chance to

171

hear what they were discussing. After a while there was the sound of a whistle and the officers walked slowly back to their cars.

I had to act quickly. Behind me was a small office, a cubicle belonging to the foreman of a maintenance crew. It was deserted, but on the wall, almost within arm's length, I saw the blue cap of a conductor hanging from a nail. I stuffed my beret into a pocket of the overalls and reached for the cap. It was a little tight on my head but it made me look like an official. A railroader. The train began a rumbling start. I grabbed the toolbox and jumped aboard the last car.

The human brain is a remarkable instrument. I knew exactly what I was going to do. The sequence of what was to come rolled effortlessly through my mind not unlike a moving picture. There was a flatcar right behind the engine's tender. I had seen the AA gun mounted on it as the train entered the station. The flatcar was the hub of my plan. I had to get to it as quickly as possible but it was way out in the front of the train while I was almost at the opposite end. Some thirty cars separated me from the target, filled with a whole regiment of SS whose sheer mass would slow down my progress through the cars. There was no time to lose.

I could feel my heartbeat accelerating as I entered the first car. Unnecessarily, I soon found out. The conductor's cap worked like a charm. None of the soldiers paid any attention to me. An occasional fleeting glance, that was all.

I entered the next car. The same thing. My confidence began to mount. It was going to be easy. One more car, and another, and still another. Everything was going smoothly. Not a hitch. Not a word. Not a question. I kept up my speed. The increasing engine noise indicated I was approaching the front of the train. My watch showed I had about thirty-five minutes left to execute my plan. In thirty-five minutes, I had calculated, the train would reach the bridge. It was the only bridge left standing to connect that part of the country with the main trunk lines running through the Rhône Valley and on to Marseilles. I was going to blow up the bridge and cut the only railway link with the south. It would take months to repair the structure, especially if the RAF hit in daytime what the Nazis could repair under cover of night.

Thirty minutes to go and I entered the last car that separated me from the AA gun behind the tender. Success had made me a little lightheaded but when I opened the door I sensed a different atmosphere. It was not an ordinary car. It was a first-class coach, the staff car.

A guard was standing inside, steel helmet, rifle, bayonet. He looked at me sharply and for a moment I was afraid. I knew if I couldn't fool him the whole thing was in jeopardy, not only the plan but my life as well. But once again the conductor's cap saved the situation. The soldier relaxed visibly and stepped back just enough to let me pass into the corridor running alongside the individual compartments.

Night had come while I had trekked through the length of the train. The compartments were dark by now and the curtains drawn. The officers had gone to sleep. As easy as that, I thought happily.

My joy was premature. The last compartment was not dark. The door to the corridor was ajar and I heard voices as I approached. The officers I had seen in Toulouse were playing cards in the cosy enclosure. The air was thick with smoke, the floor littered with empty wine bottles and cigarette butts. I hoped to pass undetected, but when I stepped into the beam of light escaping from the compartment I came into the field of vision of the officer nearest the door, a captain. He looked up, startled.

"What are you doing here?" he bellowed in German. The others raised their heads in curiosity.

I smiled apologetically.

"Nix sprechen deutsch," I said in broken German, trying to show as much respect for authority as I possibly could. I was petrified. I had to find a valid excuse, plausible enough to explain my presence, or the game was up. I saw he was searching for an appropriate word in French but I saved him the trouble. My subconscious had come to the rescue.

I pointed to the curtains, trying to make him understand I was supposed to see that the windows were blacked out. It was a reasonable explanation. He must have known the RAF took delight in bombing military trains.

For some reason, however, he did not seem completely satisfied. He stared at me strangely and I didn't like the expression in his face. As if he were trying to remember something which eluded him. I avoided his stare and busied myself as innocuously as I could without over-reacting. I had seen his eyes, pale blue, cold, and frosty. The eyes of a killer. He stood up. He was about a foot taller than I and had the build of an ox.

"Who told you to do this?" he asked in bad French.

"Orders, Herr Hauptmann," I said. It was the best answer I could think of and it turned out to be a good one. Each race, each nationality, each branch of mankind is conditioned into certain behavior patterns. Genetically rooted probably. The Germans of his generation had been conditioned to respect orders. I told him I was obeying an order which was language he had been programmed to understand. One does not question orders.

He relaxed and sat down again but it was obvious his mind was not entirely on his cards. Neither were his eyes. I sensed them following my movements while I was fiddling with the curtains and shades, driving in a tack here, fastening the tissue to the frame there. I think I did a convincing enough job while my mind raced ahead. Time was running out. I hadn't counted on this delay. The train, now speeding through the night, was fast approaching the bridge and I still had to get out onto the flatcar. I decided to put an end to the performance. Pretending I was through with the windows, I stepped over his outstretched legs, said "Pardon" as politely as I could, and left the compartment for the corridor where I looked ostentatiously at the windows, a maneuver that was to lead me to the door separating me from the flatcar. I was still within earshot when I heard him.

"I know this fellow," he said. "I have seen him before."

"Sure," said one of the players. "I have seen him too. In Toulouse. He was waiting for the train. He's all right."

"No," the captain insisted. "I've seen him before. Somewhere else. I don't like it. There is something wrong."

"Cut it out," yelled another. "Cut it out, Otto. You're always seeing ghosts. Watch your cards. You are playing a lousy game."

One of the players laughed out loud and threw his hand down. "Four aces," he said. The game was over.

"I know him," he insisted. His brows contracted.

Of course he knew me. I had recognized him the moment I saw him. I had good reason to remember him, but it was amazing he would recognize me as well. The man must have had a photographic memory. He had seen me all right. Just for a fleeting second, and that had been nearly two years before in the small burg north of the demarcation line where a few hotheads had sniped from the roofs on a German convoy. The Nazis, in reprisal, had lined up all the men of the village and shot every tenth. He had ordered the executions.

I saw that he was still trying to remember the circumstances in which we had met and I knew it was only a matter of time, perhaps minutes, for him to lock his memory into its proper place. I couldn't afford to wait till that happened. I had to get out of the coach.

He stood up again and leaned against the frame of

the compartment door from where he could watch my exit to the flatcar. Less than twenty minutes left.

Luck returned to me. The gun was not manned, nor was there a guard on the flatcar. I had to work with double speed. The antiaircraft ammunition was piled up in a semicircle around the cannon. I tore a corner of the protecting canvas off the shells and in a matter of minutes I had shoved a "cigar" deep under the bottom of the pile and searched for my lighter to ignite the fuse at the proper time.

He took me by surprise. I hadn't even heard him. In fact I hadn't heard anything, absorbed in my work as I was. The noise of the engine, combined with the howling of the driving wind, had deafened me. Suddenly the beam of a flashlight blinded my eyes and I looked up with a start.

I couldn't see him with the light in my face but I sensed his presence in the frame of the door to the staff car.

"What are you doing there?" he yelled over the din.

"Nothing, Herr Hauptmann," I shouted back. "Just resting." I could have kicked myself for my stupidity. In the tension of the situation I had lowered my guard. I had answered in German.

"I knew it," I heard him say. "I knew it! I never forget a face!"

I was still crouched on the planks when he jumped onto the flatcar. In his jump he drew his Luger and fired the moment his feet connected with solid ground.

As if to compensate for the mistake that had prompted my predicament, my mind operated with the precision of clockwork. The war, my training, the prolonged silent battle undercover had honed my senses and sharpened my reflexes. He had landed on the canvas sheet I had discarded to get at the ammunition. At the instant his feet touched the sheet, I pulled it from under him, sending him sprawling. His shot was not completely wild.

I felt the dull impact at the inside of my left thigh. Blood began to run down my leg. I could feel it, but there was no pain—not yet.

Still crouched, I charged and as he was struggling to his feet rammed my head into his stomach. He reeled backward and stumbled.

"Schweinehund! Dreckiger schweinehund!"

Those were the last words ever spoken by Captain Otto before he fell head first through the gap between the staff car and the flatcar. Then I heard a crunching sound as the wheels cut into his steel helmet. It was only much later that I remembered his head had been bare when he went overboard.

The flashlight had disappeared with Otto but the gun was still where he had dropped it. It was lying on the canvas reflecting the light of the moon. I shoved it into my pocket. Eight more minutes by my wristwatch. The wound began to throb and my breath came in short pangs. I could feel my heart thumping way up in my throat. My fingers were trembling uncontrollably when I started working again on the fuse, frantically trying to choose the necessary length to compensate for the time loss caused by Captain Otto's interference. Satisfied at last, I lit the end, watching the flame's spluttering progress for a few seconds before I grabbed the toolbox for the climb over the top of the tender. My leg began to hurt viciously.

A guard was leaning in the corner of the cab, keeping an eye on the engineer and fireman. The two—thank heaven—were French, and they looked up in undisguised surprise when they saw me sliding down from the coal. I told them in French to uncouple the engine from the flatcar because the train was going to blow up any minute. They hesitated. The presence of the guard had an inhibiting effect. It was a good thing the soldier didn't know French but he sensed something out of the ordinary anyway and raised his rifle. Through the pocket of my overalls I shot him twice with Captain Otto's Luger. He dropped the rifle and staggered and I pushed him out through the side door of the cab before he had had time to collapse.

This helped to persuade the two railroaders. The fireman crept back across the top of the tender the same way I had come. He disappeared from sight as he dipped behind the piled-up coal to uncouple the engine from the rest of the train. As soon as his head reappeared, faintly silhouetted against the sky, the engineer opened the throttle. The engine, freed of the train's cumbersome burden, jumped forward. We raced toward the bridge and reached it. The speeding engine swayed precariously from side to side on the vibrating tracks. We were going so fast we were across the bridge in a matter of minutes. I bent through the porthole and craned my neck for a look behind.

All of a sudden there were fireworks. The night lit up in one brilliant flash. The blast occurred almost dead center in the mile-long span and the train was going down the gaping hole ripped open by the exploding ammunition. It was a drop of more than three hundred feet.

"Stop the engine," I said, "and let's get out. But first help me bandage my leg."

It took us more than four days to reach the place that had been my destination from the outset. We moved at night and slept in the daytime. Farmers fed us along the way.

"I thought they had gotten you too," Henri said when I finally faced him. "Glad you made it." He had already written me off.

I smiled, as much as the pain in my thigh permitted, and handed him the cigar box.

"The cigars, mon Colonel. One is missing."

He looked at me and I knew he was wondering what I meant, but then his glance drifted to the two railwaymen who had kept back in the shadows and a big grin lit up his face.

"Don't tell me," he said. "The bridge?"

I nodded and his grin deepened, smoothing the hard lines of his face. He stepped forward and embraced me with the force of a bear. Something made him hesitate. He retreated one step and reached out for my forehead. Then he saw the blood stains.

"You are wounded," he stated. Turning to his men he ordered me put to bed without delay. A call went out for a doctor.

Later, in my delirium, I saw the face of my brother, gentle and warm, as I remembered it. Superimposed on it was another image, the vision of an endless row of railway cars filled with crawling vermin, crashing into a bottomless pit. An occasional flare shot skyward like a fiery tongue.

14

Albèrac

I had hardly been back on my feet when all hell broke loose again in France.

In the streets of Bordeaux four young Frenchmen shot and killed Hans Gottfried Reimers, a major in the German army. Reimers had been notorious for his sadism and the whole of the occupied city was elated to see him dead. The Nazis retaliated with lightning speed, however. Reimers' body was barely cold when they rounded up a hundred hostages, shot fifty on the spot, and jailed the rest pending orders from General Stuelpnagel, the German commander-in-chief of occupied France.

Simultaneously, the occupation forces received orders to shoot every armed Frenchman on sight, which was the beginning of an unprecedented open season on civilians. A harmless hunting rifle, hardly powerful enough to shoot a duck, became a pretext for immediate execution. Civilian death figures mounted, as did arrests and disappearances. Soon it was impossible to keep track of the numbers. All over the country the net tightened, threatening the limited amount of freedom of movement I had thus far enjoyed and without which I could not operate. In the general upheaval the Nazis accidentally stumbled on another pipeline relay and several of our best men were killed in the process.

Henri summoned me to Agen. He had changed visibly and the strain showed in his face. The grooves running from nose to mouth were much deeper now and the shadows under his eyes more pronounced. The loss of St. Jean de Luc and *Josephine* as a consequence of Colette's rescue had been a heavy blow. The latest incident made the damage worse, but the human flow from the north did not stop. Henri had worked frantically to keep the pipeline open. No wonder he had aged.

I had been out of action for some time after the bullet was removed. I was still limping, which did not escape the wary eyes of Maréchal de Logis Albèrac, who had taken an unwelcome interest in me. I said it was chronic sciatica which always flared up when the weather turned damp and cold. I couldn't very well tell him I had been shot by a Nazi officer while blowing up a German troop train.

Henri and I had just finished eating in our customary meeting place and he was deep in thought. After a while the wrinkles on his forehead smoothed out—a sign he had made a decision.

"We need to improvise and we have got to do it quickly," he said. There are more than a hundred people stuck at the moment at different places. The longer they

180

are stuck the easier it is for the Boches to pick them up. We have to move them and I can see only one way— your place at Lavallière. We've got to use it until we get organized again."

"It's not a good idea," I said. "I am much too exposed. Albèrac is sitting on my neck. He's been waiting a long time to get me and he's getting impatient. He is bound to notice the increased traffic in a place as small as Lavallière. Besides, he hates my guts."

"In that case you'll have to neutralize him," said Henri.

Colonel Henri was a professional soldier. In his terminology, "neutralizing" meant killing the man since it was doubtful Albèrac would yield to any milder form of persuasion. It would be an easy thing to do because of his habit of roaming the countryside after nightfall trapping people in search of a few eggs or a bag of potatoes in the farming area. It wouldn't be hard at all to ambush him in the dark. But there was also a powerful reason not to kill him.

"No good," I said. "I don't mind doing it, it would be a pleasure getting rid of the bastard. But it would stir up too much trouble. We can't afford to have more Gestapo snooping all over the place. The effect would be worse. It would focus attention on us—which is the last thing we need at the moment."

Henri considered the argument but did not seem impressed. He may have been too weary to make a hard decision. Instead, he used the time-honored practice of passing the buck. It is called delegating authority.

"I leave it to you," he said. "Use your own judgment."

And then he said something that brought back to me the memory of Sidi-bel-Abbès and my last talk with another colonel. "Démerde-toi, mon garçon," he said after which he rose abruptly and left. Démerde-toi, mon garçon. The French military man's favorite recommendation: "Get yourself out of the shit!"

On my return to Lavallière, three things happened almost at once and all three complicated the situation, although each in a different way.

First there was a message that I was to go to Marseilles without delay to clear a "shipment" for which we had waited impatiently a long time. I was relieved it had arrived but the timing was bad. I was needed here. Henri was sure to start sending a steady stream of humanity through the pipe almost immediately. The Marseilles trip would take at least a week.

The second had to do with Maria. She seemed strange. Aloof. Very detached. Not that usual vivacious self that made coming home to her such a precious event. Despite my preoccupation with matters of life and death, I was wracking my brain for an explanation of her unusual attitude. However, she removed any further need for guessing as soon as we were alone.

"I'm pregnant again," she said simply.

"Are you sure?"

"Two months overdue," she replied.

Maria was as regular as the sunrise and sunset. You could set the calendar by her. If she said she was two months overdue it meant she was pregnant. There couldn't be any doubt.

"Good," I said.

"Is that all you can say, you beast?" she said and I took her in my arms and kissed the tears from her eyes. Later we celebrated in our own way, which prompted her to say that she was certainly going to have twins.

"I'm sure you scored again, you pig. I've never seen you so wild. I'm ripped to shreds inside," she said, snuggling up to me. Seconds later she was asleep.

The third incident occurred in the morning when a gendarme knocked at the door and told me Albèrac wanted to see me right away. Ordinarily I would have taken my time but with Henri's new scheme I didn't think I should take unnecessary chances. It was better to humor the bastard instead of antagonizing him. I preferred stringing him along to being forced to "neutralize" him.

Albèrac was sitting in his cubbyhole in front of an old desk. "I want your sauf-conduit," he said as soon as he saw me.

"On whose instructions?" I asked.

He flared up immediately. "I don't need instructions from anyone," he shouted. "I am acting on general orders! You are a foreigner. Foreigners are not allowed to leave their place of residence."

Unfortunately, that was true. After the assassination of Reimers at Bordeaux, Vichy had ordered stringent restrictions on the movement of foreigners. While the regulations hadn't been strictly enforced on former soldiers, I was on shaky ground for more reasons than one. My sauf-conduit was a phony. It was an excellent forgery and indistinguishable from the real thing, but it was a forgery all the same and wouldn't stand up to closer scrutiny.

However, in a pinch I could turn it over to Albèrac, deal with him according to Henri's instructions, and get another sauf-conduit as soon as Albèrac was out of the way. But his death would jeopardize the pipeline. It would also make me the most likely suspect. Our feud was known to too many people. It was better to stall or bluff. If it didn't work I could still fall back on Henri's idea.

"You know I need the permit for my livelihood," I said.

"I am not so sure," he said.

"What do you mean?"

"Never mind," he said hastily. "Just hand it over."

It may have been a slip of the tongue, but it indicated either that Albèrac wasn't as stupid as I thought or I had not been careful enough covering my tracks. Either he doubted my travels were all in the line of business or he had somehow noticed that most of my absences coincided with some trouble in the region. The thought flashed through my mind that I would have to go through with Henri's instructions after all. It seemed the only solution to the Albèrac problem. But as far as I could tell, he was just suspicious at that point. He had no hard proof or I would have been behind the bars of his lockup.

"You are overstepping your authority, Albèrac," I said. "The paper was issued by the Prefect personally. You have no right."

His face turned red.

"I don't give a shit who issued it," he shouted "the Pope, the Prefect, or the Queen of Sheba. I want that sauf-conduit. Just hand it over or I'll throw you in the cooler and let you rot there till doomsday!"

"Don't be an ass, Albèrac," I said. "You can't go against the Prefect. He's your boss. What do you think he might do if someone told him Maréchal de Logis Albèrac doesn't give a shit about his instructions?"

"I don't give a shit about that either!" Pushing back his chair so hard it crashed into the wall behind, he jumped up. We stared at one another. I grabbed the receiver on his desk telephone. "Operator," I yelled into the mouthpiece, "Operator! Give me the office of the Prefect in Montauban. Quick! This is urgent!"

There wasn't a sound in my ear because the only woman at the town's telephone exchange hadn't even had a chance to come on the line but Albèrac couldn't know that. He suddenly changed his mind. Controlling himself with great effort, he reached for the receiver and taking it gently out of my hand, replaced it in the cradle. The bluff had worked.

"All right," he said. "I'll go through channels and get a written order and when I get it you will turn the sauf-conduit over to me. You understand?"

I nodded.

"You may go now. But you are not to leave Lavallière without my permission."

That was out of the question. I was needed in Marseilles. I had to push him one step further.

"Sorry, Albèrac," I said. "I have urgent business out of town. I'll be back in a few days. Is that all right with you?"

He was undecided. He probably thought I was planning to skip town.

"All right," he said. "But this will be the last time. And you better come back. Think of your wife and child."

He shouldn't have said that because now it was my turn to see red. I felt the blood shoot into my face and I needed all my willpower not to hit him. Only the thought of the consequences stopped me.

"Albèrac," I said, choking down the rage with difficulty, "if you so much as touch them I'll kill you. I swear!"

He turned red again. "Are you threatening me?" he yelled.

"Yes," I said and went to the door. Two of his men were standing in the frame. They had heard every word. I knew them. They were both older men and had little sympathy for Albèrac. I pushed past them.

Jules, my first mate on the *Josephine,* was sitting in my kitchen drinking coffee when I got back to Lavallière. It was a pleasant surprise. Henri had sent him to help in the pipeline operation. I had had no idea what had become of Jules after we scuttled *Josephine* near a lonely coastal stretch not far from Bordeaux. It had been heart-breaking to sink the boat but the Nazis were looking high and low for her and her crew. Jules, in due course, had reported for duty to Henri and that was why he was now sitting in my kitchen slurping my precious coffee.

There were no problems in Marseilles except for a few

sticky moments when the customs official in a sudden fit of efficiency became too nosy. The shipment had come on a Portuguese freighter consigned to Père Canouette's toy factory, labeled a special, lead-free paint which was not available in France. Four crates, each with a dozen square paint cans.

The sticky moment came when the customs man insisted on prying the lid off one of the cans, which caused me to sweat profusely. But he was satisfied when he smelled the murky paint, and cleared the shipment without any further hitch. If he had stuck his pencil into the gooey mess he would have found a false bottom only two inches below the surface. Underneath, carefully preserved in thick grease, were the parts of a dismantled M-3, successor to the tommy gun of the U.S. army, including enough ammunition to match the weight of a large can of paint.

I had to wait two more nights for the return trip. There was only one train each week because of the shortage of coal. I made sure the paint shipment was going with me. I wanted it safely under Père Canouette's roof. Henri could pick it up later.

Marseilles was swarming with German soldiers and I kept out of sight. I wasn't so much afraid of the military, but it stood to reason the Gestapo was strongly represented as well. Some of them might have seen a certain poster with my picture on it and the caption "Wanted Dead or Alive." Oran wasn't too far away.

In the early morning of the day of my departure, I was roused from my sleep by an infernal racket. My hotel was in one of the side streets leading away from the old port and there was another, almost similar hotel just across the street. When I peeked cautiously through the window of my fifth-floor room, I saw the street below teeming with German soldiers in full battle outfit. People, mostly women and children were being dragged screaming from the hotel into the street and loaded like cattle onto waiting trucks.

At the height of the commotion a window almost opposite mine flung open and a woman hoisted herself up on the sill. She had two small children in her arms. Two men behind her were trying to drag her back inside but she tore loose and jumped, clutching the children against her body. She fell like a stone. I heard the dull impact as the bodies hit the pavement.

I was told later that the hotel was used as a temporary detention camp for the families of several hundred French Jews held in a nearby concentration camp. The camp was being emptied and the inmates shipped to the east for disposal in the gas chambers. Their wives and children were being dispatched at the same time.

Henri's speed was admirable. The crates had hardly arrived in Lavallière when an old farm wagon drawn by two horses pulled up at Père Canouette's. I was left with four cans of paint and for two nights in a row Jules and I were busy assembling the guns, although we had never seen an M-3 before. Jules had only handled the French army's vintage subs and I was more familiar with the British Sten which I had used at Narvik. But we managed. The M-3 was beautiful, weighing just nine pounds and capable of firing a hundred rounds a minute. It gave me a marvelous feeling to cradle the thing in my elbow. It made me realize how naked I had been without it.

Henri was not as lucky. His gun specialist had been picked up by the Germans in the last raid on the pipeline, so he sent word through to me to come to Agen to instruct his people on how to assemble the subs. He needed them badly for a special assignment. I had an uneasy feeling about going, perhaps a premonition. Albèrac hadn't shown his face in several weeks and I did not like the calm. I knew he hadn't given up and there was only one logical explanation why he had not bothered me: he was having me watched. If that was the case it was done cleverly. I was unable to detect any sign of surveillance.

Henri had several mechanically minded men at his hideout and it didn't take long to instruct them. When I was sure they could do without me, I left. I had spent the night at a small inn. It was almost midnight when I returned for a short rest before returning to Lavallière. I was tired. I felt the burden of three years' ceaseless fighting and had also been on the go for the last few weeks without letup. My bones were weary.

The fatigue dulled my senses and dampened the caution that had become my second nature, or I would have paid closer attention to the two men who stood near the entrance of the hotel engrossed in talk.

I had hardly closed the door of my room behind me when there was a rap on it. I did not move. When I heard the impact of a shoulder against the door, I realized Albèrac was up to his old tricks. Damn him, I thought; I had acted like a goddamned idiot.

The room was on the second floor, the window just a few feet above the ground that sloped up to the back of the house. I jumped out, followed a dark lane to a dimly lit street and ran. Shades of Oran, I thought, when I heard the tramping of feet behind me. I ran as fast as I could and soon the wound in the left thigh began to throb. I was running blindly with no idea where I was going. Back to Henri was out of the question. It would blow him sky-high, and the whole group with him. I could see the domino effect in my mind. One relay blowing up after the other.

A name popped into my head: Blanchette! Strange how long a thought or a name can lie dormant in the recesses of your mind and suddenly, without deliberate prompting, emerge at the right moment from the subconscious. I had met Blanchette shortly after returning from Africa. She worked in a library and had helped me

188

find a book I wanted. After that we had a few lunches at Henri's favorite restaurant and once she had taken me to her place. She lived alone. Her mother was dead and her father, a former politician, was on the run from the Nazis.

I remembered the street where she lived and changed direction. My breath was giving out. The three flights up to her flat nearly choked me. The leg hurt. I knocked at her door while the noise below indicated I had been spotted entering the building. It seemed an eternity before I heard her voice.

"Qu'est-ce qu'il y a?" She sounded half-asleep.

"Quick, Blanchette," I whispered. "Let me in."

She recognized my voice and opened the door a few seconds later. I stumbled in.

"I'm in trouble. The Nazis are after me," I panted, hardly able to speak.

At the time France, and life in France, was full of surprises, unpleasant surprises mostly, which was probably the reason she took the instrusion in the dead of night so calmly. She listened for a moment to the sounds outside, which now increased in volume.

"Quick," she said, dragging me to the bed.

I climbed all the way back to the wall and she covered me rapidly with her blanket while she stretched out beside me, turning off the light. The blanket was over my head and I had a hard time breathing. Outside, the sound of booted feet and banging on doors. A confusion of voices. They were checking all the flats of the tenement. The knock on Blanchette's door came. She let them knock three times before she sleepily called out:

"Yes? Who is it?"

"Police!"

"Police?" she repeated, and the surprise in her voice would have fooled me under normal circumstances. I hoped it would have the same effect on them.

"Open up!" They were getting impatient.

"Just a moment. Let me get something on."

She switched on the bedlamp and reached for her gown. I squeezed deeply into the space between the mattress and the wall to get as level with the surface of the bed as I could. Quickly she draped the blanket into inconspicuous folds and unlocked the door. She opened it all the way so that the two men outside could take in the whole room from where they stood. Her attitude sounded natural. There was nothing to indicate she had anything to hide.

"What is it?" she asked.

"Have you heard or seen anyone?" asked one of the men.

"Yes," she said. "I heard you breaking down my door. What's the idea? Do you know what time it is?"

The man did not answer. He craned his neck and scanned the room.

"We are looking for a man," he said.

"What has he done?" asked Blanchette eagerly. He ignored the question. His partner was already banging on the next door.

Blanchette remained standing in the open door until the men had checked every flat in the hall, finally disappearing on the stairs on their way to the next floor. Then she closed the door noiselessly and came back. Without a word she lit a small alcohol burner and within minutes the aroma of coffee filled the room. We remained silent until the cacophony in the building had come to a climax with the banging of the front door as it closed.

Blanchette switched off the light and I undressed in the dark. She did not speak but her warm body was close to mine in the narrow bed.

Forty-eight hours later I was back at Lavallière. I had stayed in Blanchette's flat while she took a message to

Henri. He sent me another bicycle. I could hardly get back to the inn to claim the one I had left behind when I checked out through the window. The pipeline had functioned well in my absence. Not at full capacity but in drips. Each night people arrived, usually alone, sometimes in small groups. Jules looked after the mechanics. We put them up in the cellar for a day or two and fed them as well as we could, after which they would be picked up. Everything happened at night. During the day the place looked as normal as any other house in town.

I never knew the people who picked them up, nor did I know where they were taken or how. It was all part of the drill. The less you knew the less you could spill if they caught you, even under torture. The pipeline owed its longevity to this rule. The Nazis were pretty good at extracting information. When a group of Macquis ambushed a Gestapo post near Lyons they rescued a victim who had just been interrogated. His crotch was a bleeding mess and he died a few hours later. They had cut off his testicles to loosen his tongue.

Albèrac hadn't made a move since I had returned from Agen, although he must have known what had happened there. I was certain he had had me watched. He was bound to come across a lead some day which would take him straight to the pipeline. I sent a message to Henri telling him about my fears and asking him to stop shipping people—at least temporarily. He replied that I was seeing ghosts and that the Agen episode had shaken me up. I was imagining things. He couldn't shut off the pipeline. Too much depended on it.

He was right—I knew I was getting panicky and I knew why. It was the presence of the two women and the child that influenced my thinking and stoked my imagination. I tried to analyze the situation calmly and came to the conclusion that there was no danger at the moment, at least no more than at any other time. I had a fixation with Albèrac. I knew that too. My mind had blown him up beyond proportion and I even dreamed about him.

I couldn't dwell much longer on Albèrac, however, because suddenly events began to speed up. For the last two days my cellar had been crowded. Almost a dozen people had arrived but they were dispatched one by one. Finally there was only one left, a French general who had escaped from a prisoner-of-war camp and who was now on his way to join De Gaulle. Special arrangements had been made to get him across to Algeria.

The day had been unpleasantly cold and wet and dusk came early. Just before the light faded, Maria came down into the cellar.

"There is someone in the back," she said. "I think it's the old man with his wagon. I couldn't see too well from upstairs. It's too dark."

There was a small courtyard in the back of the house, walled in and sloping down to the banks of the Garonne. I doubted Maria had seen correctly. There wasn't enough space between the wall and the embankment for a wagon. But when I opened the back door I saw she had been right. The old man was there and his cart and his two horses, precariously close to the rushing waters of the river. In the dim light I saw the contours of an oblong bundle on the planks of the cart.

"Give me a hand," said the old man as soon as he saw me. "He's half dead."

"Who is he?" I asked.

"An American," he said. "A flyer. Shot down three days ago. He's got it in the guts."

I called Jules and together we lifted the wounded man from the wagon. He was heavy and in pain. It wasn't easy to get him down into the cellar through the narrow staircase. I went out to find Dr. Charron.

The doctor was an old man called out of retirement when the younger men were drafted into the army. His two sons had been killed at Sedan on the same day and just a few hours apart. I knew I could trust him. He dropped everything and came with me. After he had examined the wound and given the patient a shot of morphine, he remained standing beside the cot, apparently deep in thought.

"Not much hope," he said after a while, "unless we get him on an operating table."

We climbed the stairs. Maria had a mug of coffee ready for the doctor and he sat there drumming on the table with his fingers.

"If he doesn't get surgery he'll be dead in twenty-four hours," he said. "I have to get him to Toulouse to my brother's clinic. We'll use my car. I'll pick him up at midnight. Get me a man to help." Dr. Charron was the only person in town permitted to drive a car and entitled to a meager weekly ration of gasoline.

"You aren't allowed to travel after dark," I said. "You know that."

"I'm a doctor," he said. "I can transport an emergency case."

"Not if he's wearing an American uniform," I said. "They'll shoot you on the spot."

"I'll take the chance," said the old man. I walked with him to his office.

On my way back I passed Moulat's place. Two gendarmes were just dismounting from their bicycles and leaning the machines against the wall. On a hunch, I thought I might be able to find out what Albèrac was up to and followed them inside. They were sitting in a corner waiting for their wine. I took a chair at the table next to theirs. I knew both men. One was the pleasant-faced, roly-poly type. His name was Marinaud. The other one was lean and dark with a Charlie Chaplin mustache. They belonged to the old guard and I knew from the village gossip that they weren't exactly enamored of Albèrac, especially not Marinaud who had been in line for promotion as commander of the Vallenne post when Albèrac was appointed to it.

I said "Bonsoir." Marinaud gave me a friendly look, so I thought I should take the cue.

"Miserable day," I said, hoping to get the conversation going. "Bad weather."

He didn't answer immediately but looked at his companion. I thought the other gave him an almost imperceptible nod.

"Oui," said Marinaud. "Bad weather. Cold. But it won't last long. It's going to be hot tomorrow."

"Yes," said the other, "very hot."

I was puzzled. This was February, one of the wettest and most frigid months of the year in that part of Europe. It didn't get hot in February. Never. Was he pulling my leg? Was it a joke? Marinaud seemed to guess what I was thinking.

"Unusually hot for this time of year," he added, and suddenly I realized he was trying to tell me something he couldn't say openly. In a flash the meaning became clear: he was warning me.

There was another exchange of glances. Then the one with the mustache got into the act.

"Heat is a funny thing," he said. "Some people suffer more from it than others."

"Oui," said Marinaud. "Some people really do."

"I see," I said. "Then it's a good idea to get out of the heat if you can't stand it."

"Oui," said Marinaud. "It's a good idea, don't you agree, Jean?" The other nodded gravely. "Naturally," he said.

I had understood, but there was one more piece of information I needed.

"Any idea when it's going to warm up?" I asked.

"Early morning, I would think," said Marinaud. "About five is my guess."

I emptied my glass and put some money on the table.

"Thanks for the weather report," I said on my way out. "Perhaps some day I'll be able to do something for you."

"Who knows," said Marinaud. "Anything's possible in this crazy war."

I told Jules. "I don't like it," he replied. "Looks like Albèrac has called in the Gestapo. He wouldn't get out of bed at that time of morning. It's their specialty. They are like machines. The book says five o'clock; they'll be here at five o'clock. The trouble is they mean business. You can fool Albèrac; he is an idiot. But you can't fool them."

I agreed. This called for a change of plan. I made a quick head count—we were seven, including the two women, the child, the general, and the wounded flyer. It would be a tight fit in the doctor's car but I thought we could make it to Toulouse, where the American would be dropped off and where I could get in touch with the next leg of the pipeline. It was now my turn to be shipped through. Leaving at midnight would give us a headstart of five hours. We could be in Toulouse before daybreak and before the alarm was out.

I was busy burning papers when the doctor's wife came in. She had bad news: the doctor had run out of gas. There wasn't a drop in town. He had gone to a nearby village on his bicycle to get some from another doctor. It meant a delay of several hours. The flyer moaned on his cot. It was well past midnight, a little more than four hours to the five a.m. deadline. The general sat on a chair, his face impassive, quietly smoking his pipe. Jules looked at a photograph, his sweetheart probably. The flyer mumbled unintelligible words in his delirium. The women were asleep upstairs. I paced the floor. Waiting became unbearable. I had to do something to break the tension while we waited for the doctor. We carried the flyer upstairs to the level of the street to save time for the getaway. A mattress was spread out on the tile floor of the front room to make him comfortable.

So far the general hadn't said a word. He knew I was in charge and his soldierly training would not permit him to interfere. He was content to take orders but he also knew we were in a tricky situation and I am sure he was nervous, although he did not show it. Jules was as calm as ever.

I brought the M-3s from the cache under the basement floor and checked them quickly. Each man took one. There was enough ammunition to go around. It was now two in the morning. The minutes continued to tick by and still no doctor. The front room faced the street with the door in the center flanked by two windows. The door had a glass pane protected by wrought iron lattice work. I posted the general and Jules at each of the windows. I had no idea what made me do it, except that I wanted to give them something to do to make the waiting easier. Perhaps it was another premonition . . . or just plain luck. I remained behind the front door. The rain had stopped and a brisk wind was breaking up the clouds which scudded across the sky. The moon came out intermittently from behind the shredded clouds, throwing spasmodic light onto the street.

Another hour went by and still no trace of the doctor. I wracked my brain for a solution. Two more hours and the raiding party would be here. What was I to do, get everybody out now and try to get away on foot? Abandon the American? Wait and fight it out, three against I don't know how many? And how about the women and the child? My head was spinning crazily. Time was running out.

At three o'clock the decision was taken out of my hands. It was the one and only time in all the years I had dealt with the Nazis that they deviated from their five o'clock rule.

At three o'clock sharp a car came careening down the street.

"The doctor," whispered Jules.

The car came to an abrupt stop in front of the house, brakes screeching wildly.

"No," said Jules. "That's not the doctor. He wouldn't drive like that."

I peeked through the curtain behind the wrought iron of the door. It was not Dr. Charron. The light was just strong enough for me to see a small German army truck that held eight or ten men. It was loaded to the hilt.

Heavy boots began to break down the door. I jumped back as the wood splintered and the glass broke. The door flung open. I flattened out against the wall.

But no one entered. Instead, I heard a voice.

"Out!" screamed the voice. "All of you. With your hands up over your heads! On the double!"

It was Albèrac. I knew his voice and his dry, hacked Corsican accent. Jules had been wrong on two counts. He had said Albèrac wouldn't be getting out of bed in the dead of night. Well, Albèrac was here now. Secondly, the Nazis had come at three. Jules had said they never came before five. I meant to tell Jules he had been wrong but it wasn't the proper time for that. Instead, I took one step forward into the frame of the wide-open door. Albèrac was standing some fifteen feet away, revolver in hand, which he raised as soon as he saw me. I didn't give him time.

My M-3 burped softly a few times. It pumped at least twenty bullets into Albèrac's chest. He collapsed in slow motion like a deflated balloon. Henri would be pleased that I had neutralized Albèrac after all.

Simultaneously, the general and Jules started shooting at the truck. It happened so quickly the Nazis hadn't even moved. Before they could scramble from the open seats they were hit. An M-3 fires a hundred rounds a minute and the moon was our ally.

Albèrac had not been alone. Another officer dove for cover under the truck, but I shot him several times before he could wriggle out of sight. He lay still. I ran out into the street but there was no need for more shooting. The fight was over. It had lasted hardly more than thirty seconds. They hadn't fired a single shot. I counted ten dead Germans.

We hauled the corpses from the vehicle. There was no time to wipe away the blood. The flyer was loaded and wedged between the two elongated seats of the truck. By the time we managed to get the heavy body up and in a secure position, the women were downstairs. Maria had François strapped to her back and carried two small bundles. Mother was very pale but seemed calm. Lights were coming on in the windows of adjacent buildings, when Jules revved up the engine. Wearing Nazi steel helmets we raced out of the town on screaming tires. It wasn't too effective a camouflage but camouflage all the same.

Albèrac was lying on his back in the street, his eyes open.

15
Finale

In some places the snow was knee deep, in others there was only sheer ice underfoot. Another craggy peak loomed ahead in the darkness, slightly softened by the snow's luminescence. The plodding was tough and grew tougher as the hours went by. It was two in the morning.

We climbed in single file, Manolo, our Spanish guide leading the way. Either he knew the mountain well or he had an inborn sense of direction that let him find his way without hesitation through petrified mazes of rock and ice in uncompromising darkness. Jules was behind him, followed by Maria, who had François strapped to her back in a leather contraption. Manolo had offered to carry the child but Maria was adamant. Although dead tired she refused to give up the child and nothing I could say would have any effect on her. I couldn't help her. I had my hands full supporting Mother, who was near the end of her endurance.

This was the last leg on the road to Spain and it was the toughest. We had now been under way for five hours and there was no end in sight. The mountain still stood before us, blocking the path, gigantic, dark, menacing. It was hard to believe only three days had passed since the episode at Lavallière and the mad drive to the border. The distance from Lavallière to Perpignan was only about a hundred miles but I had been forced to take the side roads for fear of running into roadblocks which had effectively doubled the distance.

I had taken the wheel from Jules. My mind was crowded with tumbling thoughts as we raced through the night at a crazy clip. There wasn't enough time for elaborate plans so I had to improvise. Trying to make it to the clinic of Dr. Charron's brother was out of the question. I had no idea where it was located in the first place and driving into Toulouse would be insane. I prayed that the flyer would hang on until I could get him to a surgeon or a hospital somewhere. I skipped Toulouse and headed straight for Perpignan, to the south and close to the Spanish border.

Some time before Henri had given me a contact in Perpignan as insurance toward a day of need which had now come. The contact was the man in charge of the last link, the tail end of the *tuyau,* the final relay in the pipeline. Henri had impressed on me to use him only in extreme circumstances. If it was blown too the only remaining escape route after the loss of *Josephine* would be blocked.

Despite unfamiliar roads and the darkness of night I made good time. Jules navigated while the general sat in the back, his arms around the two women to steady them in the crazily swaying vehicle. The flyer was still. Perhaps he was dead.

At dawn Perpignan came into view. I knew the town had a large German garrison because of its proximity to the border. To drive in was tantamount to suicide. I slowed down before reaching the outskirts on a stretch of road flanked by cyprus groves and clusters of the mushroom-shaped pine trees of the Midi. I found a spot where the trees bunched together into a thicket and drove the car into it, meandering around tree trunks, finally stopping where it couldn't be seen from the road. I left Jules in charge and walked into town. I knew that Armand, my contact, owned the only bus in Perpignan allowed to shuttle between the town and Prats de Mollo, the last French outpost in the Pyrenees. I had been told to look for the bus at the railway station.

The station was swarming with German soldiers. It looked as if the whole occupation force had converged on Perpignan but for once I didn't mind. The more the better. Fading into the milling mass reduced the danger of detection.

I found the bus. A young man was sitting in the driver's seat, smoking.

"Monsieur Armand?" I asked.

He shook his head and pointed with his thumb to the door of a bistro across the square.

"He's in there," he said, "eating breakfast."

I recognized Armand. He had been at Lavallière a few times to pick up some of the more important people in the human cargo that passed through my cellar. But he had never told me his name. The less you knew, the less you could spill. The recognition was reciprocal.

I quickly briefed him. He was sharp and intelligent. It showed in the few questions he asked, and then he said I should relax and eat something and wait for him. He was going to be busy for a couple of hours. When he returned he said the flyer was still alive and had been taken care of. The general was already on his way to Port Vendres, a short stretch down the coast, where he was going to be smuggled aboard a fishing trawler for the trip to North Africa. Jules and the women were waiting for me at Armand's place a short distance away. When I got there, everybody was asleep.

Armand left for his run up to Prats de Mollo. He returned shortly before midnight with the latest news. What I expected had happened: every German post along the Spanish border and all Vichy police had been alerted with strict orders to shoot me on sight. They had even dug up the old "Wanted Dead or Alive" poster. But Armand said there was little danger from the picture. It didn't do me justice. I had grown a sizeable mustache in the meantime, which altered the likeness considerably. But all the same Armand was not satisfied. He went out again and came back with a bottle of black hair dye. When he was through with me even Mother did not recognize me at first.

Armand was a native of Perpignan. He knew the mountains well and he was thoroughly familiar with the routine of the Nazi garrison. When he explained his plan to me, I accepted without question. His bus ran once a day up into the mountains to the tiny resort of Prats de Mollo. It was imperative for us to get there, he explained, as it was the key point for the trek across the Pyrenees. The only mountain pass negotiable with relative safety at this period of the year was accessible only from Prats de Mollo. Anywhere else the terrain was too dangerous. Avalanches would bury us in no time at all.

"There is one hitch," he said. "The road to Prats is heavily guarded all year. Ordinarily it doesn't affect me except for the occasional spot check. But now with word out that you'll probably try to get out from this end, they'll step up the watch. As a matter of fact they already have. There's a way out but it's risky."

I couldn't help grinning at the word "risky" and I saw the question in his eyes.

"Risky?" I said. "What do you think the last five years have been? Wine, women, and song?"

It was now his turn to grin. He went on.

"There is a checkpoint half way up and just outside a small hamlet. That's where they are now searching the bus. It's the only danger spot on the road to Prats. It means you can't go with me. But there is another bus, smaller than mine, that goes only as far as the hamlet. They never bother with it. At least they haven't so far because it doesn't go as far as the border. You follow me?"

"Yes," I said. "And I suppose you want us to take it."

"Exactly. You take it to the hamlet and continue on foot up the road. There is only one road; you can't miss it. I'll catch up with you as soon as I've cleared the checkpoint. Once past it, they always leave me alone. There's no further check.

In the morning everything went as planned. Armand had found a collapsible pram and we strolled out of the small cluster of houses with Maria pushing the carriage. We looked like a family of vacationers enjoying the mountain air, although it was hardly the season for a holiday.

Soon we reached the checkpoint and passed it. Armand's bus was stopped and the passengers lined up outside. About a dozen steel-helmeted soldiers in full battle dress were checking papers and belongings. Armand sat behind the wheel pretending not to see us. We kept on walking up the road.

We walked. The road climbed steadily, winding itself

in needle-sharp curves around the profile of the rocks. At each precarious turn the snow-covered heights of the Pyrenees appeared in their technicolor glory set against the blue of the sky. Spain was on the other side of the peaks.

We walked. Time stretched and uncertainty grew. There was no sign of the bus. Armand should have caught up with us long ago. I hoped he hadn't run into trouble with the Nazis. The incline became steeper. I felt it in my leg muscles. Two hours passed. Three. We walked, getting more weary with each step. Then, at last, there was the sound of a coughing engine below in one of the curves. After a while the bus rolled around a turn and stopped. We climbed aboard.

"Salopards! Dirty bastards!" mumbled Armand as I pushed past him. "Kept me all afternoon. Took seven people off the bus. Gestapo. Grilled me for an hour."

The inside of the bus was jammed, standing room only for the remaining two hours of the trip, with the engine laboring up the mountain at a snail-like pace. It was twilight when we crawled into Prats de Mollo and came to a stop on the tiny square dwarfed by the towering mountains.

But even the failing light could not hide the surprise that awaited us: another set of steel helmets, carbines, and bayonets. Armand had said there wasn't going to be another check. We looked at each other but he was as surprised as I. He didn't waste a single moment, however. There was a furtive and whispered conversation with several passengers next to him which quickly spread through the whole bus. Whatever the message, Armand made sure it reached the farthest corner before he pulled the lever that opened the door.

I had a good notion of what had prompted the change in their routine. They were after me. The knowledge failed to elate me. There was no way out of the trap

203

I could see and it looked like the end of the road for all of us. The Nazi soldiers now formed a solid half-circle around the only exit door of the bus. Short of a miracle the end had come.

But Armand performed that miracle. He had blocked my way while an emotional human avalanche rolled through the door, pushing and kicking against the line of soldiers, who in turn began to push and shove in the opposite direction to contain the onslaught. At the height of the commotion, a woman began to scream at the top of her voice, her face contorted. Doubling over she clutched her belly as in great pain and collapsed. On the ground she thrashed wildly with arms and legs. The bewildered soldiers, abandoning the fight, rushed toward her. Still she screamed in agony.

Armand had waited for the moment. "Now," he said. "Into the door over there!"

The bus was stopped in front of a hotel, a tall, very narrow structure. The door was open. I grabbed Maria's arm and propelled her out of the bus in the wake of another wave of passengers. Jules dragged Mother along. There were now almost a hundred people milling wildly about in the small space between bus and hotel, blocking the soldiers' view. The crowd opened a passage and we rushed through the door which slammed shut behind us. We were in luck: the Nazis hadn't seen us.

It was pitch dark inside. Someone pushed us upstairs and into a room. The guide was already there waiting for us, a short, stocky Spaniard who was to take us across the mountains the same night. But he wouldn't. He said we were not fit to go because of the unexpected delay. Much too tired. He wouldn't risk it. He would come the following night after we had had a chance to rest.

"Stay in your room," he said before he left. "Don't go outside for any reason. The town is not safe."

During the night a storm moved in and in the morning the mountains were shrouded in dense clouds. When they lifted, the peaks glittered under a fresh load of new snow. It was cold. The hotel had no coal. The water froze in the pitchers.

In the late afternoon a second storm blew in and at nightfall, Manolo, our guide, came. The trip was off again because of the weather.

But the next morning the sun rose in a cloudless blue and radiant sky. The landscape was breathtakingly beautiful, even though I wasn't in the mood for beauty. I looked out the window. The latest delay had made my nerves raw. Holed up in the room had made things worse. I felt like a caged animal. I couldn't stand it any longer. I had to get out, at least for a few minutes.

I said I was going for cigarettes. Maria objected. She quoted the Spaniard.

"Nonsense," I said. "I'll take François with me. What could look more natural than a father and son out for a walk in the sunshine?"

She was still reluctant but let me go.

I shouldn't have gone. I was hardly out on the street when I bumped into a tall gendarme who had popped up from nowhere. An adjutant. My attempt to get past him failed. He stopped me.

"Who are you?" he asked. I gave him a name I remembered from one of Henri's identity cards.

"What are you doing here?"

I tried an innocent smile. "Taking a vacation. Doctor's orders. I have a bad heart." I remembered vaguely having read somewhere of Prats de Mollo's climate and its curative qualities which were attributed to its high altitude.

He looked at me searchingly. For a moment I was afraid I had run into another Albèrac. He shifted his glance to the child, who looked at him with big blue eyes in unmitigated admiration of his uniform and then he looked back at me. He turned his head in the direction of the mountains and scanned the snow and the sky and I sensed that he was trying to assess the weather up there. He seemed satisfied with what he saw and turned to me again.

"Listen, whoever you say you are," he said. "To-morrow, first thing in the morning, I am going to check the papers of everyone in that hotel of yours. If I find you haven't got a medical certificate that says you have heart trouble I'll send you back where you came from! Do you understand?"

I said I did. He disappeared around the corner. But there was no need to fret about a medical certificate. He had judged the weather correctly. It was good enough to make it across the mountains and at nine in the evening, Manolo sneaked us out of the hotel through the back door.

Five hours had passed since we left Prats de Mollo. The plodding became painfully slow the higher we climbed. I was near exhaustion. François slept peacefully in his straps. He was doped with a sleeping pill. Mother was getting weaker by the minute: I was almost carrying her. We stopped for a rest. A half moon had come out from behind a tall peak. There was now some light.

It is still unclear in my mind if it had to do with the improved visibility of the terrain or with Manolo's senses, which were much sharper than mine, but whatever it was it saved our lives.

"Jump!" Manolo suddenly yelled. "Madre de Dios, jump!"

We jumped to the left, the only way we could. To the right was a chasm going down into the dark, dead shadows. We jumped, sliding down a short icy slope. Bullets whined over our heads. A German patrol!

We slid some ten or twelve feet before hitting the

bottom of the gully. Manolo pointed to a spot in the shadow of the moon, cast by a huge pile of rocks. Jules was the first to reach it when a voice shouted: "Halt oder ich schiesse! Stop or I'll shoot!"

The sentry was either overconfident or inexperienced—or perhaps careless from dealing with too many hapless fugitives. He made a mistake—he stepped from the shadow of the rockpile straight into Jules' path.

Jules crouched and rammed his head into the man's stomach. Gravity increased the momentum of his powerful body and the sentry went backward, dropping the Schmeisser submachine gun which clattered across the ice toward me. I picked it up.

Jules was an experienced Underground fighter. He had the sentry by the throat and pushed him toward the rim of the deep crevice that had opened before us. The sentry kicked desperately to free himself from the choking grip but his boots found no traction on the sheer ice. With an ear-piercing scream he went over the edge, nearly joined by Jules who regained his balance only at the last agonizing second. I had already seen him going down with the sentry but miraculously he scrambled back up on all fours.

Straightening up, he almost stumbled into the bayonet of a second Nazi who had materialized out of nowhere. The scene was indistinct and the shapes moved so quickly in the eery twilight of moon and snow that I realized I would be unable to do anything to prevent Jules from being killed. The Nazis themselves solved my dilemma.

There was the distant rattle of a machine gun and we all dropped into the snow, with the exception of the Nazi who inexplicably remained standing. But only for a moment. Then he collapsed. Something warm and sticky splashed into my face. With a reflex action I emptied the whole Schmeisser magazine in the direction I thought the shots had come. I don't think I scored but the shooting ceased.

The second sentry was dead. The bullet had blown apart his skull. Some of his brain and blood had splattered on my face. I wiped it off as well as I could, fighting off the rising nausea.

The Spaniard saw the mess in my face. "Madre de Dios," he mumbled, "let's go! Let's go!" and we scrambled along the path. For once the Nazis did not come after us.

The shooting had had a strange effect on me. I didn't feel tired anymore. Body chemistry, I thought. Hormones in the bloodstream. I felt them coursing through my veins, or at least I thought I did. But it took the lead out of my bones. I hoped the women were feeling the same effect.

The trek continued. After a while the fatigue returned, worse than before. Each new step turned into torture. Then, without any transition, the terrain leveled out. Manolo stopped and we clustered around him.

He stretched out his arm, pointing into the darkness. "There is Spain," he said. "Mucho suerte! Good luck!" and without another word slipped out of sight. One moment he was here, the next he was gone. How he knew we were in Spain has puzzled me ever since. I could only see the blackness of night and the ice and rocks around us.

We tramped on but there was no need to climb anymore. The ground sloped slightly downward and the snow began to disappear. After a while we hit what may have been a goat path and we followed it. The descent grew steeper.

Through the longest night of my life we kept on plodding mechanically. We must have been asleep on our feet but they somehow continued to move in steady rhythm. My senses were so dulled I failed to notice that the sky had gradually turned lighter. We stopped for a few minutes to rest. Maria dropped François gently to the ground.

And suddenly the sun was there, rising to our left from behind the craggy profile of a mountain, and in the first light of day I saw the green fields of Catalonia spread out before me.

I strapped my son to my back and began the descent into Spain. For me the war was over.

Epilogue

There are people who believe in miracles and there are others who believe in guardian angels. There are those who believe in divine power and those who profess that everything is preordained and no matter how often you act the fool or idiot, everything still proceeds as written.

I do not quarrel with any of these beliefs. Thinking back to the period covered by this book, I still cannot understand how escape was possible and I ask myself what it was that warned me to run time and again at the propitious moment. Was it precognition or sixth sense that compelled me to move? Or was it perhaps some sort of genetic instinct of the hunted passed on to me from distant ancestors who had learned to flee from forces they couldn't understand? Perhaps it was a miracle after all, a guardian angel, divine intervention, or a combination of one or more of all these things. I have no answer.

I only know I got away. How I managed it with a small child, a pregnant wife, and an old mother in tow, is still hazy in my mind even after the passage of so many years and the time I have had for reflection.

But I did escape and I lived and I became the bridge to the future of my family as its sole male survivor. It was a close call, but I lived and was able to write this book.

W.K.
September, 1978